SECRET SCUNTHORPE

Morgan Broadbent

AMBERLEY

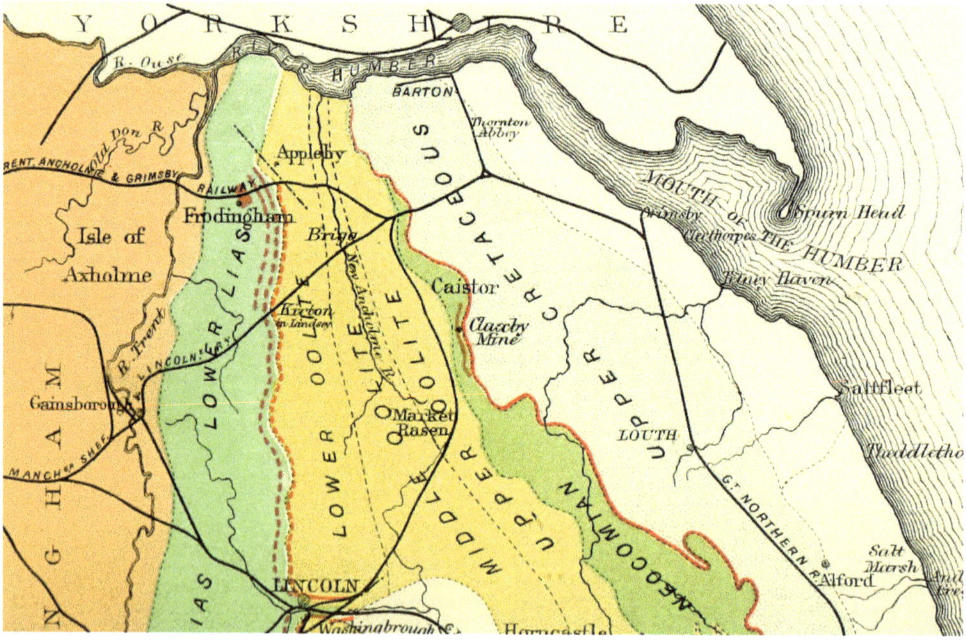

Modern Scunthorpe is located in the 'Lower Lias' blue section at Froddingham. The mouth of the Humber can be seen spreading out into the nearby Wolds of Scunthorpe, showing the tight-knit location of the villages surrounding the area.

First published 2017

Amberley Publishing
The Hill, Stroud
Gloucestershire, GL5 4EP

www.amberley-books.com

ISBN 978 1 4456 7206 9 (print)
ISBN 978 1 4456 7207 6 (ebook)

British Library Cataloguing in Publication Data.
A catalogue record for this book is available from the British Library.

Origination by Amberley Publishing.
Printed in Great Britain.

Contents

Introduction

It is perhaps, to some extent, a natural element of having lived in a certain place for a long period of time to overlook the local history of the area you inhabit. After living in Scunthorpe for the majority of my upbringing, it is clear that a town takes the form of a 'home' instead of a place you conceive as historically rich or imaginably interesting as an immediate connotation. The celebration of local historical culture has always remained an aspect I have been keen to perpetuate, but this became especially important after my first visit back to Scunthorpe after being away at university. The place in which you live brings with it a personalised identity that shapes you; attending university in the south of England made this very clear for me.

Scunthorpe today is arguably most well known for its steel industry, but the aim here is to explore elements of the town we are often unaware of or that deserve a greater amount of historical appreciation. Scunthorpe actually has a surprising history that dates back to the Stone Age, while the exploitation of the local ironstone resources is something that perhaps remains quite attached to the modern aspects of the town and its formation. The increase in the town's population in the early to mid-eighteenth century caused the expansion of Scunthorpe including the surrounding villages of Frodingham, Crosby, Brumby and Ashby. This mark of local history is still signposted with the appearance of village signs, pubs and establishment names. It seems quite comfortable to uncover the historical origins of a town before you begin to concern yourself with everything else that makes it unique. From discovering the very early history up until a modern view of the town, it is both interesting and consolidating that Scunthorpe was once never known as just that.

Scunthorpe has the often-profound reputation of being an 'industrial garden town', but this book will explore the foundations of the town's origin and the subsequent history of what we know it to be today.

When you are presented with the task of writing a book on a place you know incredibly well, the task of deciding what to include and how you should do it becomes overwhelming. A town is perceived differently by everyone: those who live there, those who know it vaguely and those who have never even visited. I have therefore chosen to structure this book in an almost chronological sense, starting with some of its earliest history. From then on the more modern aspects of Scunthorpe will be the focus, with sections dedicated to specific areas. The steel industry of Scunthorpe will, quite rightly, be a large aspect of the book, but not its sole focus. Other areas, such as the gardens of Scunthorpe, will seek to justify the town's title and embrace the local history in a way it deserves to be celebrated.

As a history student, it is mandatory to understand the importance of historical significance and what it means to become appreciative of the history you are presented with. While we often think of history to mean war, dates and events, we can therefore forget that the streets we walk upon every day are rich with history. I wanted to write to educate myself on the little-known history of my home town, but I also wanted to make these elements accessible to anyone who is interested or indeed curious. I believe that everyone should know about the history of the place they live, even if it is just something that happens to be unique or abstract. By writing this book, which has been a personal, yet very interesting challenge for myself, I hope to have made myself into a much better historian who goes out into the world to find out new information as opposed to simply studying books. But more importantly, I hope to have served Scunthorpe and those who live within it some well-deserved acknowledgement when it comes to its proud and deep history. It is not every day you are presented with opportunities to write, especially when it concerns the thing you enjoy.

1. Scunthorpe's Early History

Scunthorpe and its surrounding areas were surprisingly settled within at a relatively high rate during the prehistoric period. While the fact that Scunthorpe did increase as a relatively modern settlement in the late nineteenth century, the idea that this was the sole spurt in its trend of settlement is a misconception. Evidence has been found to support the fact that settlement may have taken place during the later Upper Palaeolithic period. As a result of most of this evidence being archaeological, other sites in the area have also found signs of Mesolithic inhabitation, suggesting that early settlement was common in many different historical periods. While this serves as a great historic interest, only a small amount of evidence has been found from these periods, though it is lucky we have found such at all.

Neolithic

The very early history of Scunthorpe begins with the appearance of Beaker folk both within the town's perimeters and surrounding Wolds. These early settlers were present in the Stone Age, and date back to 10,200 BC at the latest, though it is probable that settlers within the area were not around so far back. Bell-Beaker folk are often referred to as

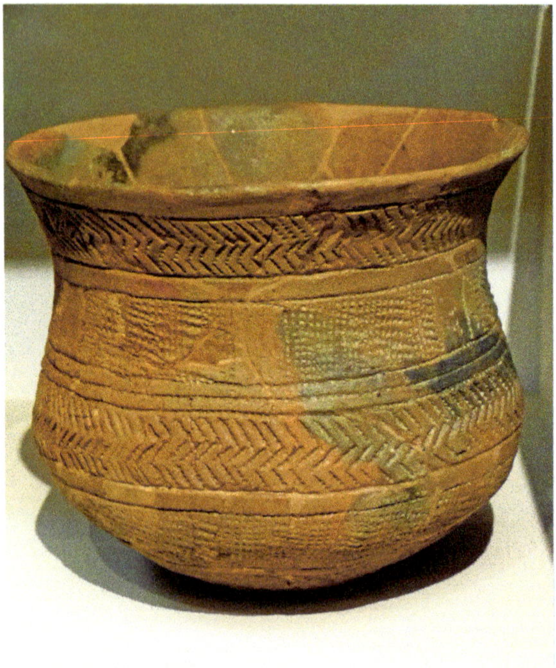

The pottery that gave the Beaker folk their unusual name.

Beaker folk and people; they are named after their unique pottery that is shaped like beakers, which is often a typical sign of their settlement. Archaeological evidence such as this pottery has helped to identify and determine their existence within the area; however items typically made of flint or stone help most in the identification process and were preserved well due to their resistant nature. Part of the reason the Scunthorpe area may have attracted early settlement is perhaps a result of the high quality of potential farmland; many of those who settled around the area seem to have a recurrence with the use and importance of farming in their daily lives. Dragonby in particular has not only produced evidence of the Neolithic period from excavations, but also from other historic periods. The appearance of beakers in archaeological excavations mark a clear distinction of the later Neolithic period.

As we can see, when we study maps of the Neolithic period, finds such as pottery are predominantly found in the eastern side of England, the majority of Lincolnshire is in fact covered by these finds and perhaps suggest that these settlers may have preferred to be near to the waterside.

Bronze Age

The Bronze Age in history is an important indicator to progress regarding production – hence the period's name being given in response to the use of bronze. The period also reflects a time of increased trade and immigration to the British Isles, suggesting perhaps the development of economic sophistication.

Work that took place during the nineteenth and early twentieth centuries revealed evidence that Bronze Age settlements may have existed in Brigg, a small market town located close to Scunthorpe. It is thought that settlement – or at least some of the discovered evidence – dates around the mid- to late Bronze Age (around 2000–1000 BC), and has included some analysis of soils and other natural materials.

Workers in Brigg found the Brigg Boat in the River Ancholme – a partially intact boat that is now situated in Hull Museum for visitors to see. But this is not the only discovery within Brigg, the Brigg Raft was excavated by archaeologists in the late twentieth century and is now looked after by the Brigg Heritage Centre, where is on display. The raft was initially discovered while workers were digging for clay, and was initially assumed to date to the Viking period. After other boats were found in the same area and placed in Hull's Maritime Museum, it was decided that the raft would be lifted; the idea that the boat was indeed Viking began to be doubted and an analysis was scheduled to occur.

DID YOU KNOW?

The Brigg Raft is not actually a raft, it is instead a boat. It was decided that the find would be named a raft in order to differentiate it from the other boats found around the Ancholme and marshes. The raft must be kept in a stable environment due to its fragile nature, though it is still on display for people to view.

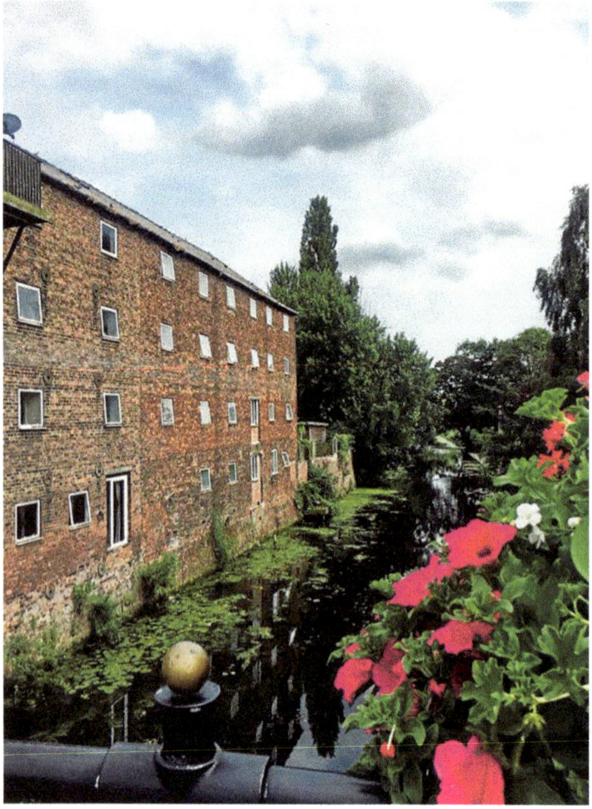

The River Ancholme was used for trade of goods and transportation.

The raft was lifted in sections due to its large size. It is one of the only Bronze Age boats to be found and also in a stable condition, and so it could be researched and put on display. The raft was moved into the Brigg Heritage Centre in an attempt to bring an influx of tourism into Brigg and the surrounding Wolds; it is safe to say that this action has certainly succeeded.

But what also helps us to identify Brigg with the Bronze Age is the timber trackway located next to the River Ancholme, helping people to travel over waterlogged ground in periods of heavy rainfall and dampness.

The trackways include pieces of bronze or a combination of materials that date back to the Bronze Age. It is interesting to consider this type of settlement during this period. Bronze was a valuable resource, meaning that Brigg must have served as a useful place to settle if those who lived there bothered to employ their material.

During the Bronze Age, Lincolnshire was seemingly an ideal place for farming settlements, particularly in the areas surrounding Scunthorpe. It is said that Brigg offered one of the best places to cross the marshy land during this period and perhaps explains why the land was found fertile for agriculture. Brigg came to be a busy market town around the same time Scunthorpe had its first boom in its population, and its weekly market that has been running for over 800 years demonstrates its strong attraction for settlement and its tradition with its residents.

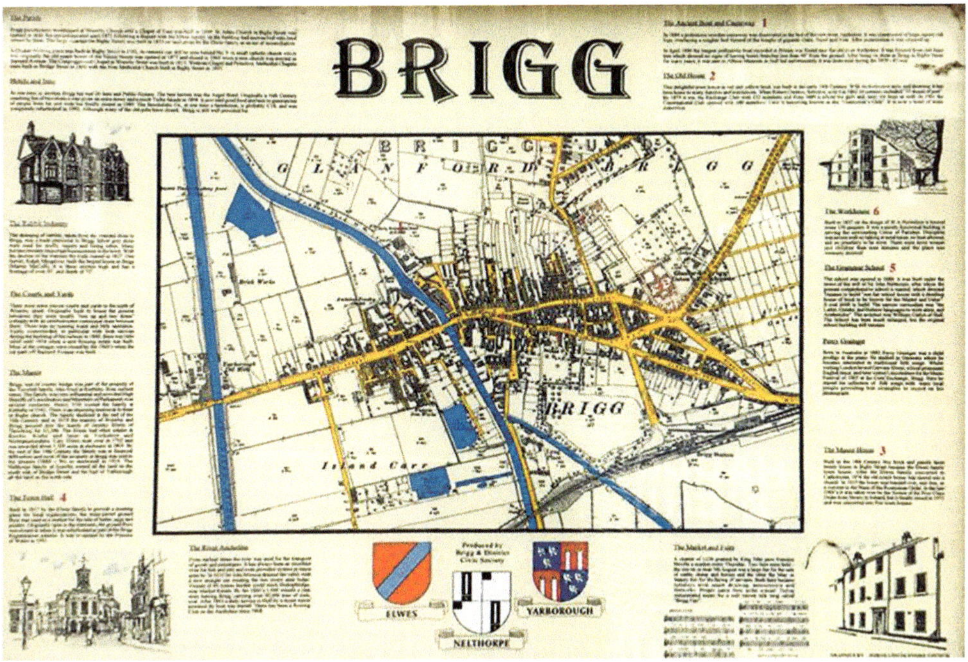

A small map of Brigg showing the Ancholme.

Iron Age

The Iron Age is perchance the most compatible period in terms of manufacturing similarities with modern production, and is the first age to date to the modern historical period (around AD 100) rather than the prehistoric. Iron became the most popular material to craft objects such as weights and household tools due to its flexible nature. Locally, the village of Dragonby is actually one of the most significant sites from the Iron Age in England due to the finds from excavations in the area. Discoveries such as pottery and the agricultural state of the soils suggest that those who lived within and around Dragonby during the Iron Age may have taken up occupations such as farming. Valuable objects – for instance, stoneware – does imply craftsmanship took place during this time in the village. Overall, the evidence from Dragonby demonstrates differing occupations may have been practised, but more importantly it shows the area was inhabited and worked well during this period.

As well as its former history, Dragonby has become rather famous locally due to the existence of the so called 'Dragonby Dragon', an accidental structure that has attracted much attention. The excess produce of a limestone spring caused the formation of the 'dragon', and the village itself is now named after the Tuffa dragon that inhabits the village. Unfortunately, the wild grass around the mound has been allowed to grow over, meaning that a modern picture of the dragon does not show it very well. The head of the dragon lies at the bottom of the structure, while the higher part at the back shows the risen spine and tail.

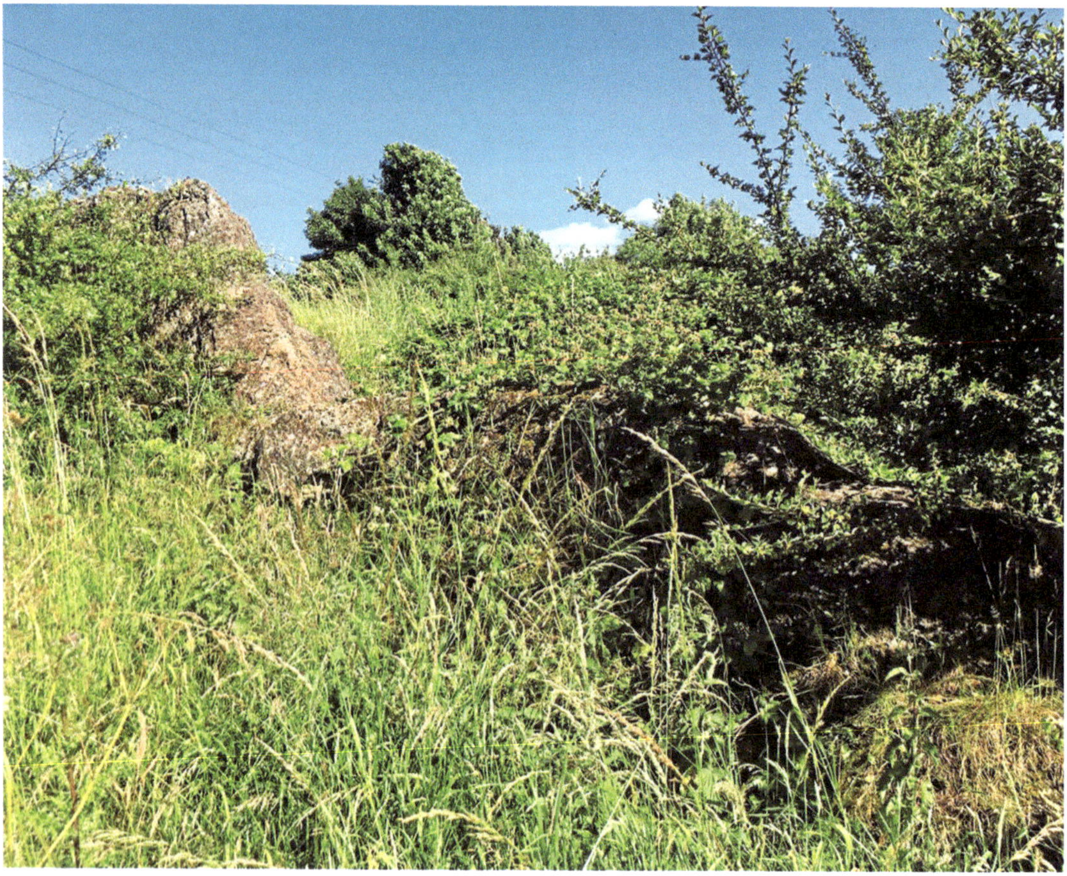

The Dragonby Dragon, which has now become overgrown.

Roman

During the Roman period, the first hints of Scunthorpe's role in the iron industry became well cemented, perhaps even laying the foundation for its modern reputation. Iron was produced in Scunthorpe on a relatively small scale to efficiently satisfy the domestic demand for produce and equipment, primarily that concerned with the farming industry that lasted up until the fifth century. The Romans lived in Britain for nearly 400 years after a series of invasions and conquering established their rule. They split Britain into sections, which is, in technical terms, referred to as civitates. Lincolnshire was known to the Romans as the Kingdom of Lindsey and became a reasonably strong regional power. Its population and prosperity meant that it survived and performed well during the majority of the Roman period, but it is important not to overstate its economic climate too much as it was never as greatly powerful as other regions.

Just to the north of Scunthorpe lies the village of Winterton. From the early second century the Winterton villa existed as a Roman operating farm and is today one of the most important sites of Roman history in England. It is especially known for the series of mosaics found within its premises (similar to those found at Horkstow villa), though

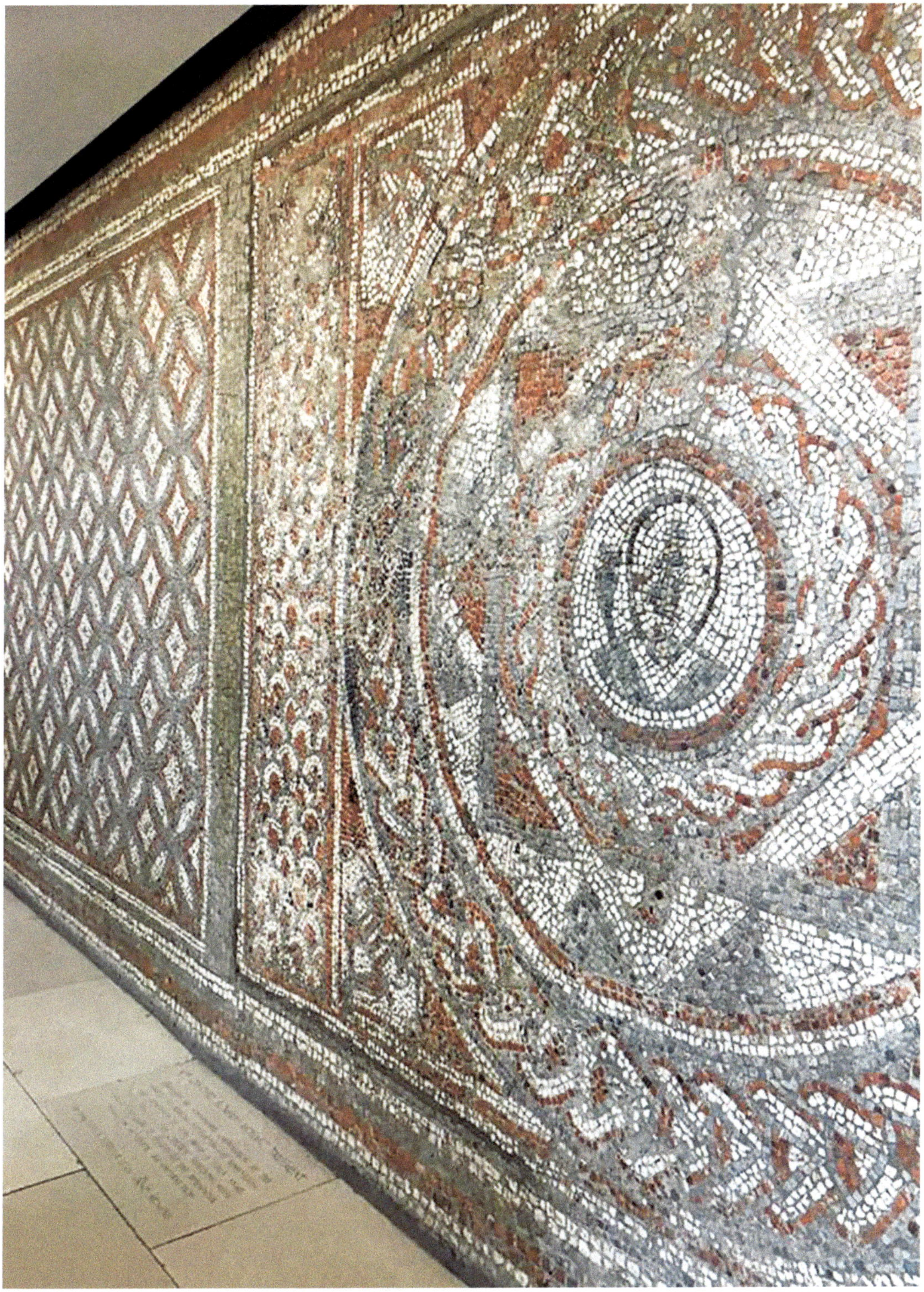

This mosaic is on display at Pitwood House.

unfortunately little is known of it. What has made this site very famous locally is the discovery of the Winterton Lady, found in 1968 during work in the area – a full female skeleton and likely one of the villa's former residents.[1] Another villa is also thought to also have existed in Winterton, however there is a small amount of evidence in comparison to the Winterton villa we are aware of at present.

Mosaics like these were found on the floors and walls of villas, and often feature unique and intricate patterns of animals and mythology. This mural, excavated in 1959, features Ceres the goddess of agriculture. The mosaic was given to the Scunthorpe Civic Centre by the Sawyer family and makes up virtually the entire back wall of the building's front entrance. Perhaps the goddess was intended to act as a symbol of luck and worship in hope that she would provide good conditions for their land. Some of the pottery and objects found on archaeological digs are also delicately designed; it has been mentioned that artwork in the villa is also of a unique nature in terms of their attention to detail.

Other areas close by are thought to have been under the Roman influence during the same period, though ones such as Hibalstow have far less evidence than that of Winterton. A well located in Bottesford, officially known as Templar's Bath, has also been estimated to date back to the Roman period, though the uncovering of the bath in the twentieth century produced little evidence. Bottesford Manor is thought to have once lead to it, as well as being associated with the preceptory thought to have been located on the land before it was likely to have crumbled and built over. Today the manor and the well are still intact and are a heritage site for visitors to enjoy.

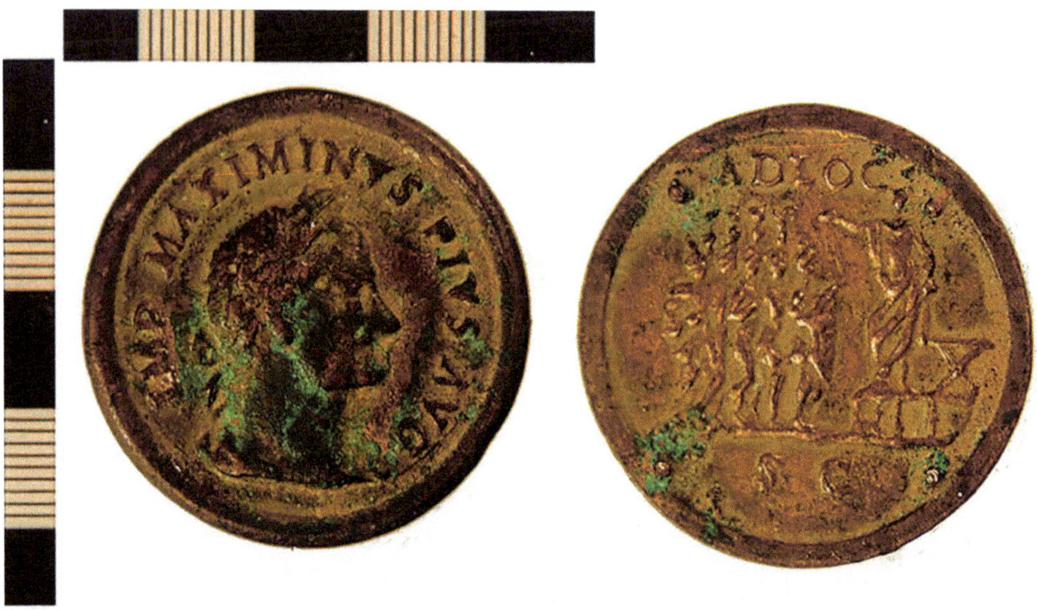

Roman coins found near Scunthorpe.

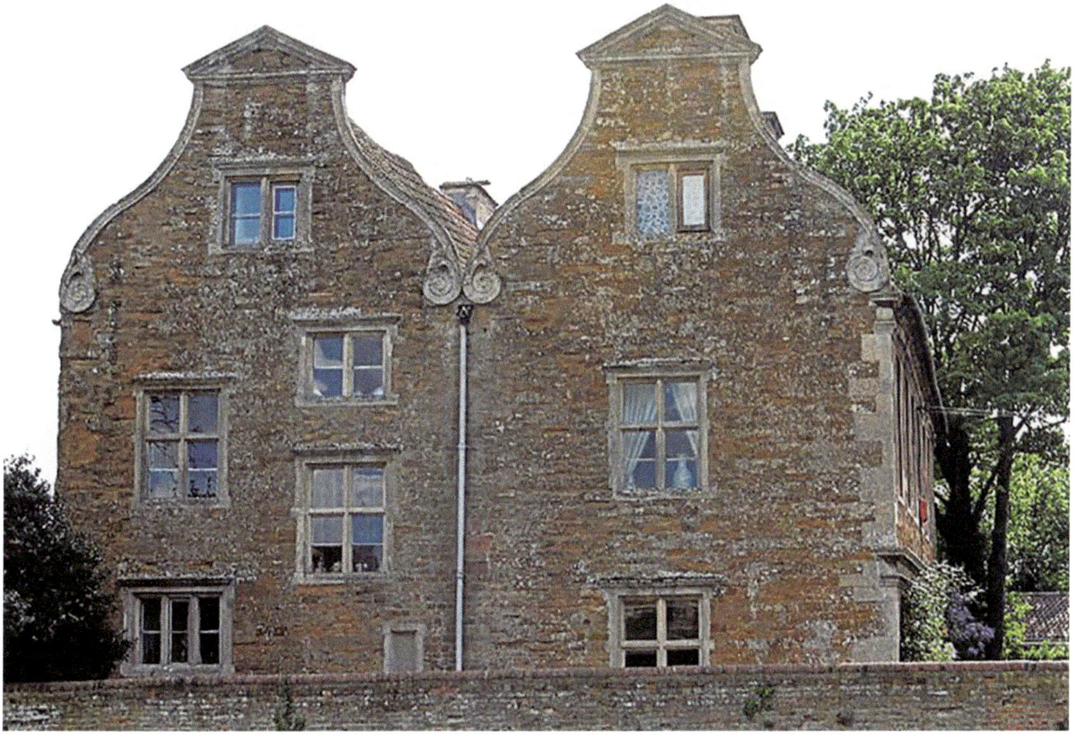

The great manor of Bottesford. (Courtesy of Jo Turner)

DID YOU KNOW?
It is widely thought that many travellers would set off to Bottesford in search of Templar's Bath. They believed that the water running from it had healing properties, so many would drink and bottle it. It is also likely that people would attempt to sell this water later, though it is unlikely that it brought anyone the benefits they desired.

The local town of Kirmington, situated today near to Humberside Airport, was known for its Roman roots during the first century, demonstrating the extent that the Romans were likely to have settled in this period. An auxiliary fort was created at the settlement after it had been used during the Iron Age. It is unknown why there is a differentiation in the amount of evidence found at different, though close locations. This may be due to a larger penetration in settlements elsewhere, such as Winterton, or perhaps instead the perishing and diminishing amount of evidence within other areas.

Saxons

The area of Lindsey – or rather, as it should be referred, the Kingdom of Lindsey – is more often a popular area of interest during the Saxon period in comparison to others. This is quite frequently due to the entire region being studied as a whole rather than small specifics being individually analysed, but the kingdom was thought to be part of a wealthy region. What may also explain the depth of research and evidence is the duration of the period, which lasted over at least six centuries from the end of the Roman occupation to the eleventh century. This means that the amount of settlement has provided much material to work with. Lindsey did eventually become absorbed into the Kingdom of Northumbria after tedious disputes and battles, but the period gave rise to some local history in the area of Scunthorpe.

Flixborough, located just to the north of Scunthorpe, near to Burton-upon-Stather, happens to have its origins as an Anglo-Saxon settlement area in the seventh century and ending in the early eleventh century.

The settlement is situated on a slight hill overlooking Scunthorpe and the River Trent. This may have made it a desirable location and ideal for its formation as the Trent may have posed as a potential threat to flooding, destroying agriculture and houses in those settlements located on the countryside flats.

Archaeological work in the area has resulted in the findings of high-quality objects that have been preserved well, suggesting a perhaps prestigious occupation within the area. This evidence, donated to the North Lincolnshire Museum in Scunthorpe, has allowed archaeologists to reconstruct an idea of the houses and other aspects of the daily life in the Anglo-Saxon era. Other sites such as cemeteries are also part of important evidence we have of the existence of the Saxon heritage in England.

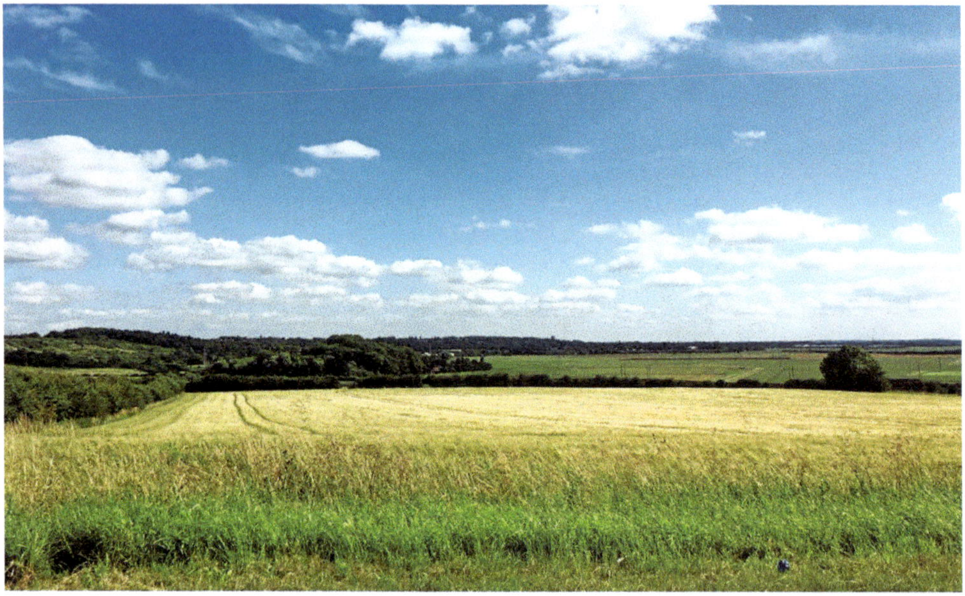

The high land is advantageous around the area.

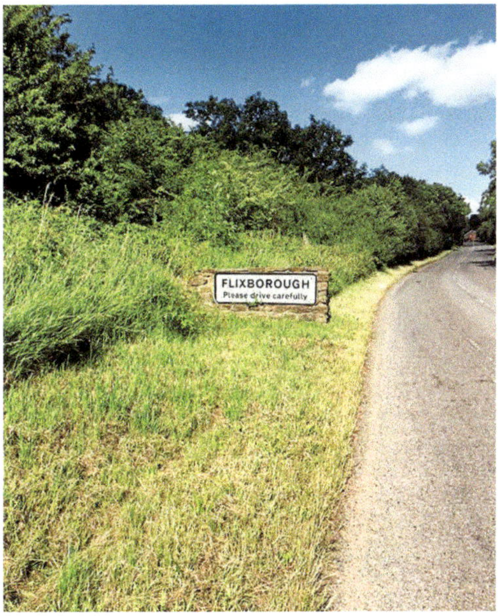

The south entrance to the village, overlooking Scunthorpe.

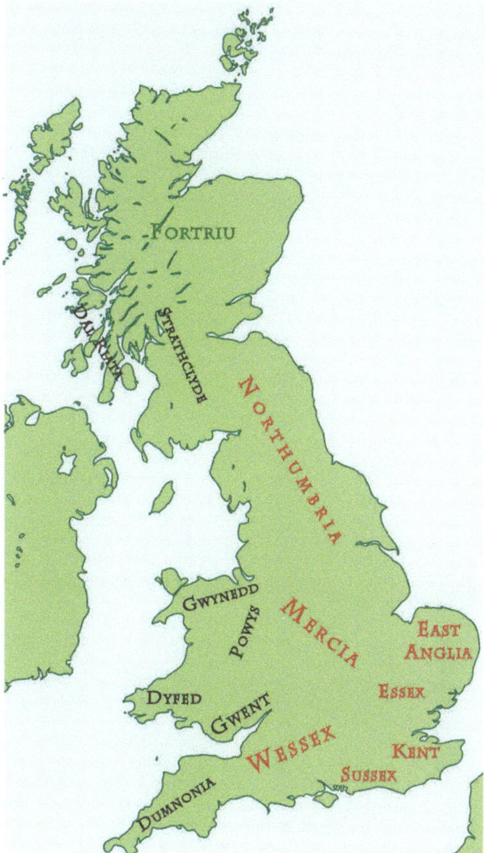

A map showing the large kingdoms during the Saxon period.

The small town of Bottesford, adjoined to Scunthorpe, also happens to be part of local Anglo-Saxon history. While it appears in the Doomsday Book, St Peter's Church is a landmark that dates back to the eleventh century. When the new church was built, evidence was found to suggest that the site of an older Saxon establishment had existed before.

Vikings

Vikings were Scandinavian subjects that ventured to England, as well as other places such as France, in search of wealth and land. The first record of a Viking attack in England was at Lindisfarne in the north of England; they later progressed to invade the rest of the country by repeatedly attacking the isles and winning the Battle of Hastings in 1066.

DID YOU KNOW?

The area that the Vikings decided to travel and plunder was often determined by where they originated from in Scandinavia. This is because it was geographically more sophisticated to attack those in close proximity, hence why some would target Iceland and eventually the Americas while others would venture into the Mediterranean.

Scunthorpe, unsurprisingly from its name, has been thought to have connections with the history of the Viking settlers. The place names surrounding the town, often including the identical suffix of 'thorpe' or '-by', are the biggest indicators beside finds in the area of settlement. In total, fifty-three place names in the north of Lincolnshire provide evidence that the Vikings partook in large-scale settlement in the areas around Scunthorpe – estimated to have been in the late ninth century.

These Scandinavian place names were not given out by mere chance, however. 'Thorpe' is to mean 'secondary' or 'an outlying settlement'. Others such as those including or, more specifically, ending in 'burh' came to mean 'a fortified and strategic location'. The 'Scun'

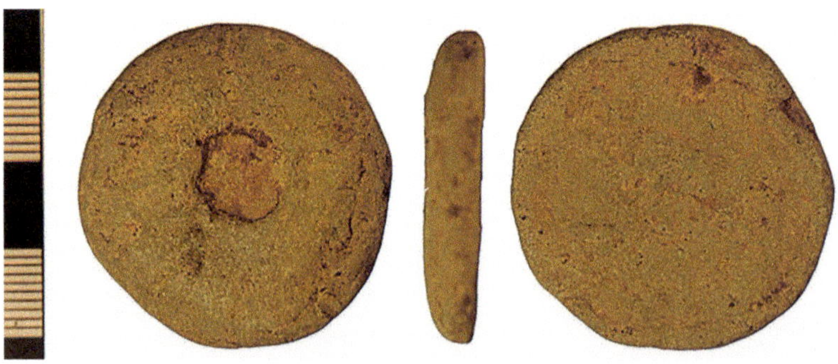

A Viking weight. (Courtesy of The Portable Antiquities Scheme/The Trustees of the British Museum)

in the name of Scunthorpe acted with its suffix to compound a translation of a Danish personal name: 'Skuma's-thorpe'.

This archaeological evidence of an imbedded weight is a sign of Viking occupation. It was found in Kirton in Lindsey and adds to the evidence of settlement within the North Lincolnshire region.

What also makes this period both useful and interesting is the existence of the Doomsday Book, which was created in 1086. As Scunthorpe appears within the text, like many other surrounding places such as Barton, we are able to establish when local sites came into existence as a form of date measurement.

Medieval

The medieval period merges with the end of the Saxon time frame and runs alongside the Viking era within the timeline of England; this is why when we look at some evidence, such as churches, it appears some have a tendency to archeologically overlap. Though many places being mentioned in correspondence to historic periods do not strictly belong within the town of Scunthorpe, they do have with them an identity of belonging within the area. Alkborough, a small village located near Winterton and Burton-upon-Stather, is another example of one of these places that is historically significant.

Alkborough was thought to be a Roman river post: it is located on higher ground, thus serving as an effective form of defence. But Alkborough's Roman roots are just the start of its curious history. Julian's Bower is the pride of Alkborough and what it is most known for. The turf maze is indeed a curiosity as its exact dating is yet to be established, although many believe it to date to the medieval period. The Alkborough Maze Committee voluntarily maintain the upkeep of Julian's Bower and provide information for visitors. The maze was first recorded in 1679.

There are many theories surrounding the mapping of the maze and what it represents. A popular and more classical theory comes from a tale of Theseus slaying a Minotaur, where wool was said to have been used from the entrance to trace his path so that once the Minotaur had been killed he would be able to navigate his way out. Others tell of Italian replicas of turf-cut mazes after the Greeks destroyed Troy, religious Christian symbols and the work of monks. The maze can also be seen on the floor of Alkborough's church and some gravestones in its cemetery, demonstrating the attachment and symbolic nature Julian's Bower has on those who live in Alkborough.

Alkborough was previously used before as a small port due to its level of accessibility on the flats, but in the last century it has also been used to raise cattle and grow crops to cater for increases in demand. The Owston Ferry Museum is an example of the agricultural and farming industry of North Lincolnshire, its preserved equipment demonstrates that, like most other villages surrounding Scunthorpe, the land was fertile and efficient for its purpose.

Gainsthorpe, near to Kirton Lindsey, is also home to another medieval treasure. An aerial view of it was recorded in 1925 in order to see the full scale of the former settlement. English Heritage look after the abandoned medieval village today. It is estimated that it was well planned out, as aerial images show heavily established grooves in the landscape. Unfortunately, it was deserted by the late seventeenth century due to agricultural and

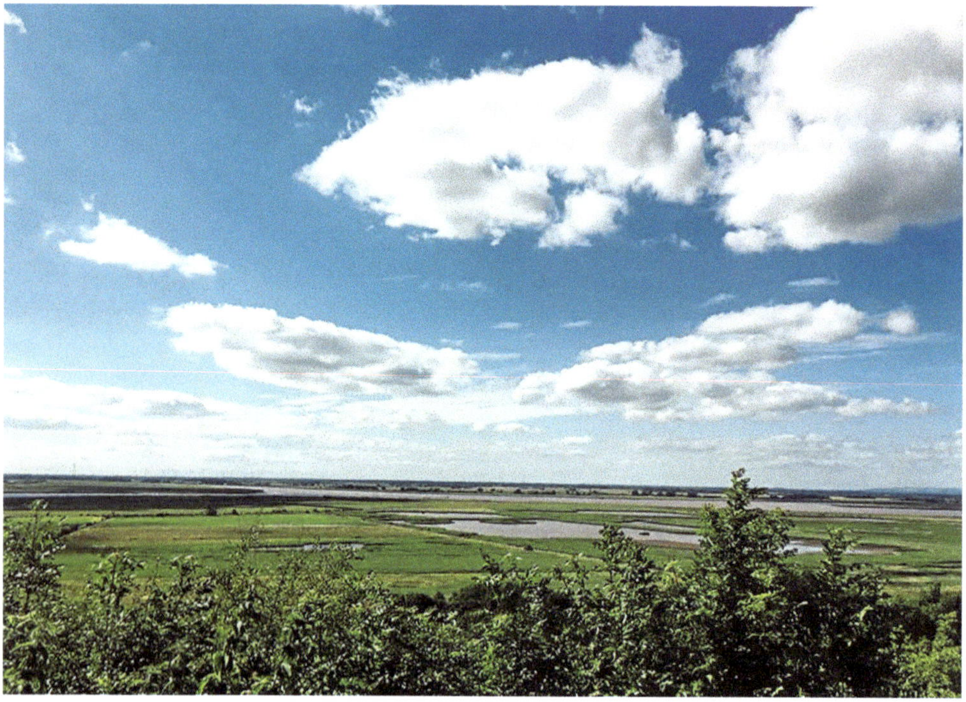

The view of the flats from the 'cliffs' of Alkborough.

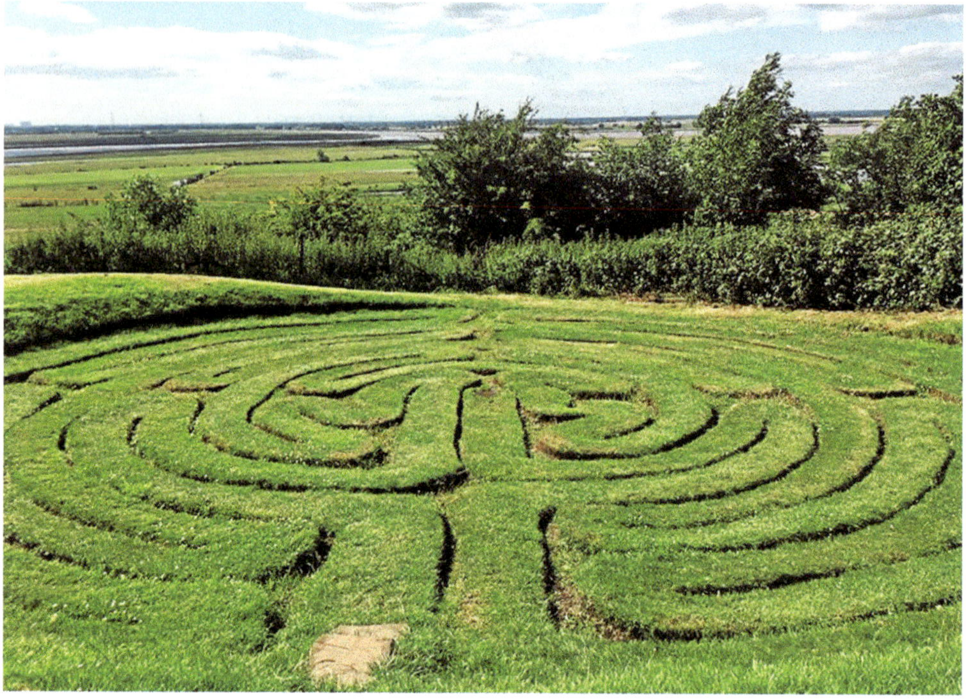

Julian's Bower at Alkborough's viewing point.

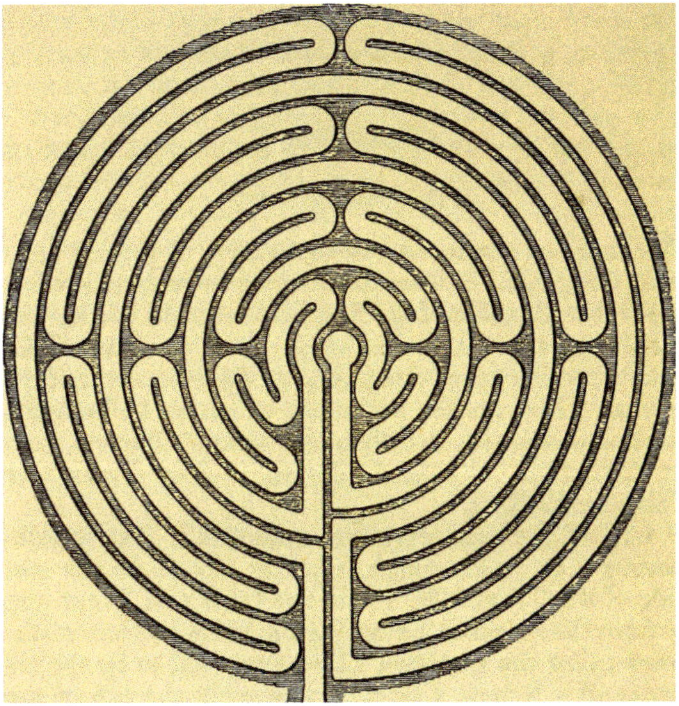

A drawing of Julian's Bower turf maze.

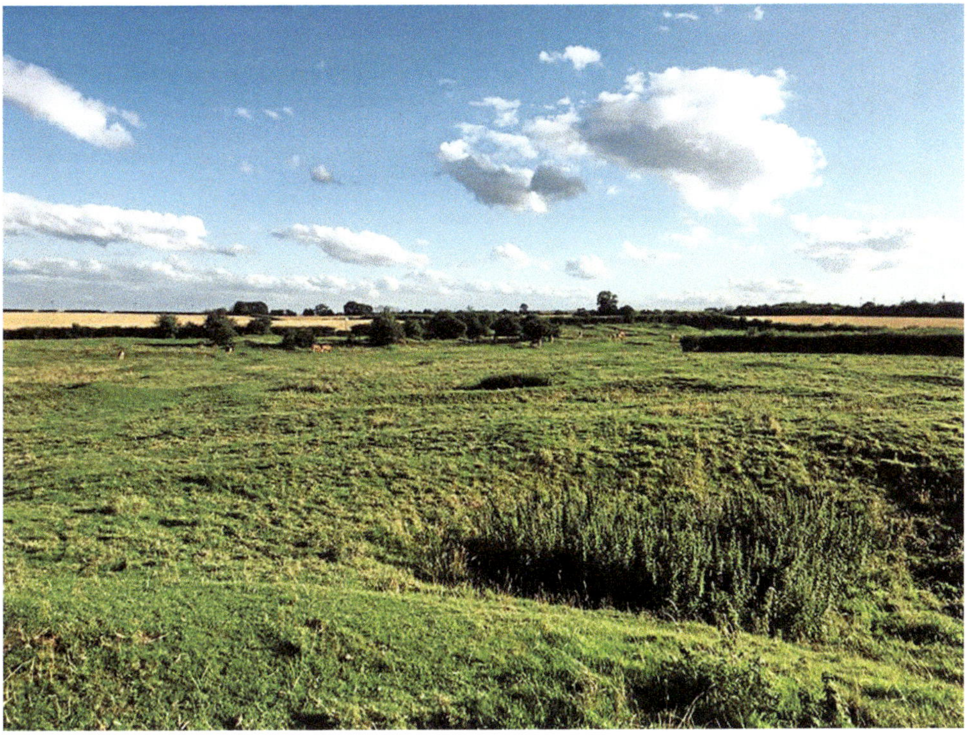

The site of the medieval village, which is protected by English Heritage.

economic changes in success, meaning that the village possibly became quite poor before its inhabitants moved on in search of prosperity. It is likely that the area of Gainsthorpe was later used as a shelter or stronghold 'checkpoint' for those travelling towards Scunthorpe and Lincoln.

It had perchance occurred to some travelling from village to village in the area that Ermine Street is seemingly everywhere. It is not true that there are multiple streets named Ermine, but instead the road stretches across such a distance. Ermine Street is a Roman road that originally ran from London to Lincoln and then to York after. While today the road has changed slightly and has different names, the part that extends to Lincoln crosses through the North Lincolnshire district. The long straight road, unsurprisingly given the local history of the area, dates back to the Roman period.

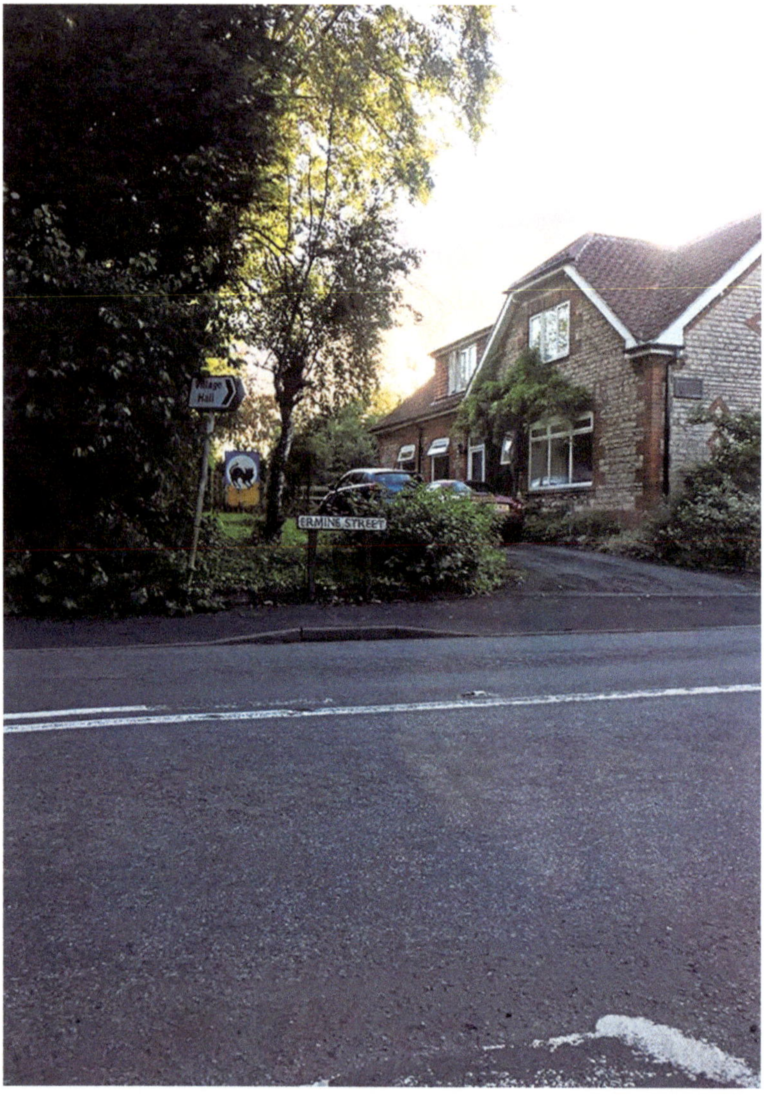

Ermine Street was likely to have been used by travellers.

2. The Formation of Scunthorpe

It is a vital part of Scunthorpe's history that we acknowledge the town was once in a state of separation and disconnectedness. When we travel around the town, the former village names have been kept in place not because there is ever a desire to be apart, but rather because Scunthorpe is a place of the united diversity of its founding villages. Most sources concerning Scunthorpe's relatively modern history date back to the 1850s at the earliest, and, even so, this is a combined mention of different sections of the parish before it ever was one. Quite naturally, the ironstone in the local area of the town were found to be extremely rich upon its discovery in the mid-nineteenth century, and were subsequently taken advantage in the process of founding the steel industry. The ironstone reserves were not exploited so much by those who inhabited Scunthorpe around its finding, but presented the opportunity to create an industry that is likely to have attracted some entrepreneurs who were seeking to make their fortune from an unlikely area. This originally began as the Frodingham ironstone industry, forming the basis for the steel production in Scunthorpe and the attraction that constitutes settlement today to the then small town.

Throughout this book, Scunthorpe is referred to as the town it is today being an entire entity, but it was once not even a town and instead just one of five small villages. I think that after living in a place for so long the idea of these villages is normalised and is therefore

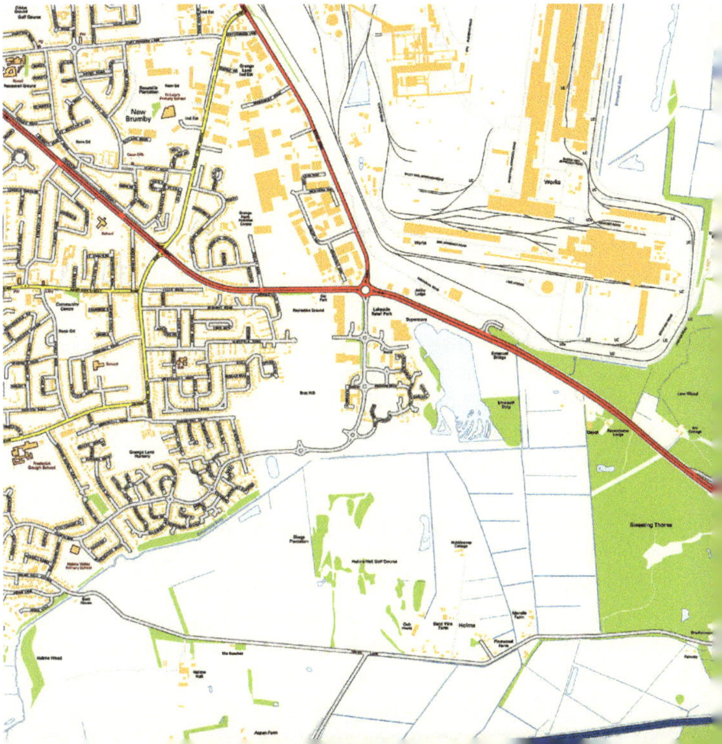

A recent map of the town, showing the development.

dismissed, but because each simply connects to one another it is perhaps more difficult to picture how different Scunthorpe once was. The village of Scunthorpe joined with those of Brumby, Ashby, Crosby and Frodingham, villages that are located nearby. Each of the 'founding' villages of modern Scunthorpe, as well as others in the local area, relied on agriculture due to the fertility of the land, and began to prosper during good seasons of farming. As a result the townships became increasingly developed, but Scunthorpe unsurprisingly took the lead in terms of its growth. This does not mean to suggest that the village of Scunthorpe was always far superior in comparison to its neighbours; the rabbit trade primarily concerning Brigg provides evidence that Brumby was involved in a sense of economic sophistication due to its trade links, but it just so happened that Scunthorpe was a large settlement. The first villages to join were Brumby and Frodingham in 1894. Shortly after their merging, the village of Scunthorpe expressed great interest in joining them, but the formation of the town did not turn out as smoothly as anticipated. The primary reason Scunthorpe had wanted to unite with Brumby and Frodingham was to incur the economic benefits in terms of sharing basic public services, making the unit cost cheaper for each of those involved. But due to disagreements and tensions between the townships, the plans were soon turned away in 1903 after they had been presented shortly prior.

DID YOU KNOW?

One of the founding villages of Scunthorpe, Crosby, was actually owned by the Sheffield family – the wealthy family who also own Normanby Hall. It is said that they ordered the building of properties and schools.

By 1912, the former village of Scunthorpe had instead joined with the remaining villages of Crosby and Ashby after leaving Brumby and Frodingham to exist as one. Crosby and Ashby had decided that the economic efficiency that would be brought by joining Scunthorpe would pay off in their favour, though it was rumoured some time ago that, despite the benefits, Scunthorpe may have bargained the others greatly in order to retaliate against Brumby and Frodingham. Shortly realising the new progress of the other villages, the latter decided they wanted to become part of the new village formation – excluding themselves would make little sense. New plans were proposed and finalised for settlement, and the villages became one just after the outbreak of the First World War due to the increased needs of industrial output.

DID YOU KNOW?

For some time Scunthorpe was not actually known solely as Scunthorpe and instead as the Scunthorpe and Froddingham district. While Froddingham was well known, the same could not be said for the village of Scunthorpe. A name could not be decided between the two.

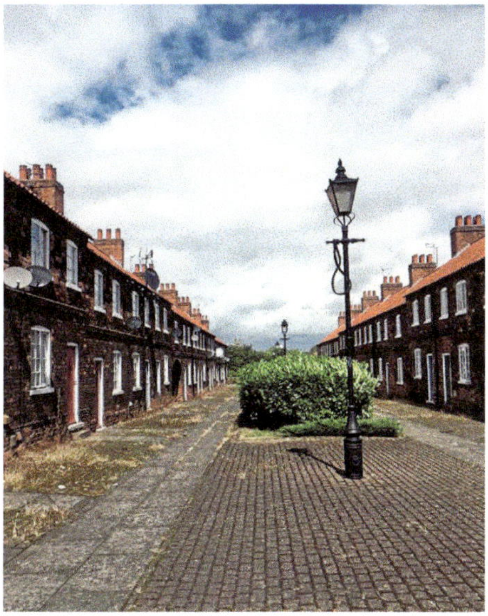

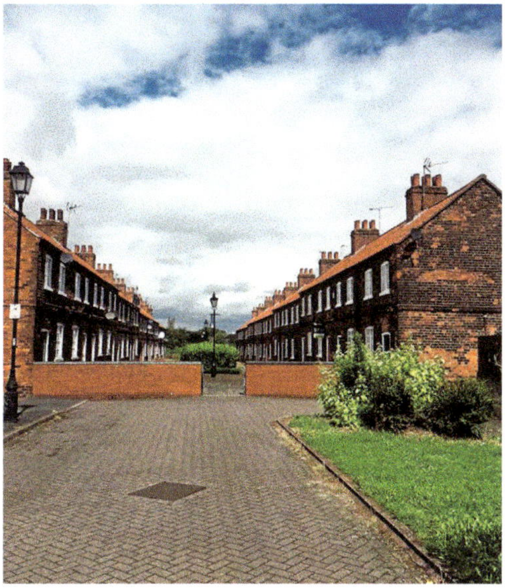

Left: These houses were rumoured to be the first constructed.

Right: Small houses located near to the steelworks.

Over time, the townships merged together to form the Scunthorpe we know today: shops were built, roads were formed and expanded, and the local economic climate began to take off. The new town was planned out carefully to avoid disruptions to those adapting to the new landscape, which involved constructing new houses in between the villages to join them together and making an accessible network to flow through each of them. It is not surprising that this was the primary period for many pubs and leisure activities to be constructed. Many of these places provided a ground for new neighbours to meet and created an efficient way to encourage social and economic integration.

While steel manufacture became important to Scunthorpe in later years, the production increased during the First World War in order to cope with the excess demand for steel to create munitions. The Lindsey Ironworks and surrounding area became heavily industrialised in the period running up to the outbreak of war and was sustained during this period. As a result, an influx of workers came into Scunthorpe to help manage the demand due to the large availability of jobs at the production sites. But these dedicated workers of Scunthorpe steel needed to remain relatively close to the production line in order to supply an easily accessible labour force on short notice, and houses quickly became high in demand around Frodingham district the small town. Throughout the war and the forthcoming years, many council and a small proportion of private houses were constructed to house these new steelworkers. Ironmasters also gave away land to provide space for houses to be built for their workers – examples include many of the houses near to Cottage Beck and Rowland Road.

It is rumoured that Rowland Road and its leading streets, such as Cottage Beck Road, were initially intended to be the main high street of the town when the area was first built. The location would have been ideal due to its close proximity to the steelworks and its population

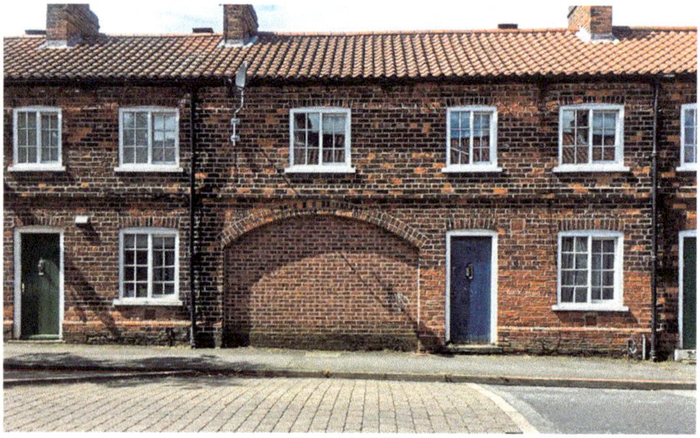

Many of these streets have filled-in horse bridges.

of workers and their families. Both roads in question lead directly to the site. What also gives a vital clue to this assumption is the width of the streets: if the area was planned to be one of the most popular in the new town, it would explain why the roads are so large.

Houses in the area were built as part of the Redbourn housing scheme and included the estates surrounding Henderson Avenue as a way to create a housing block near the steel production.

During the war period, Anderson and Morrison shelters were used by some in Scunthorpe at the time, but unfortunately many were apprehensive that they were unsuitable to be utilised properly. It is difficult to say whether or not North Lincolnshire was particularly targeted during periods of bombing and raids, but it is rumoured nevertheless that the steelworks sites and bridge at Keadby were targeted. Like most areas, Scunthorpe was bombed a few times during the war, which often damaged housing and domesticated areas. The steel plant was particularly guarded, and defence measures were put in place to stop or at the very least minimise the impact of bombs being dropped. These events were an obvious setback for the new blooming town, but, needless to say, it seems the area and its Wolds did not incur too much sustaining damage and returned to its normal development after the war had ceased.

DID YOU KNOW?

The bridge running over the River Thames often known as Keadby Bridge is actually named after George V. It opened in 1916 and began as a functioning drawbridge, but today it has been fitted to remain stable for trains and cars to cross.

Once steel production had become much more stabilised in the post-war period, the High Street and small precincts were built to supply an area for shopping and convenience. The main High Street welcomed the precinct that is today known as the Foundry, forming the most popular area to shop in the town.

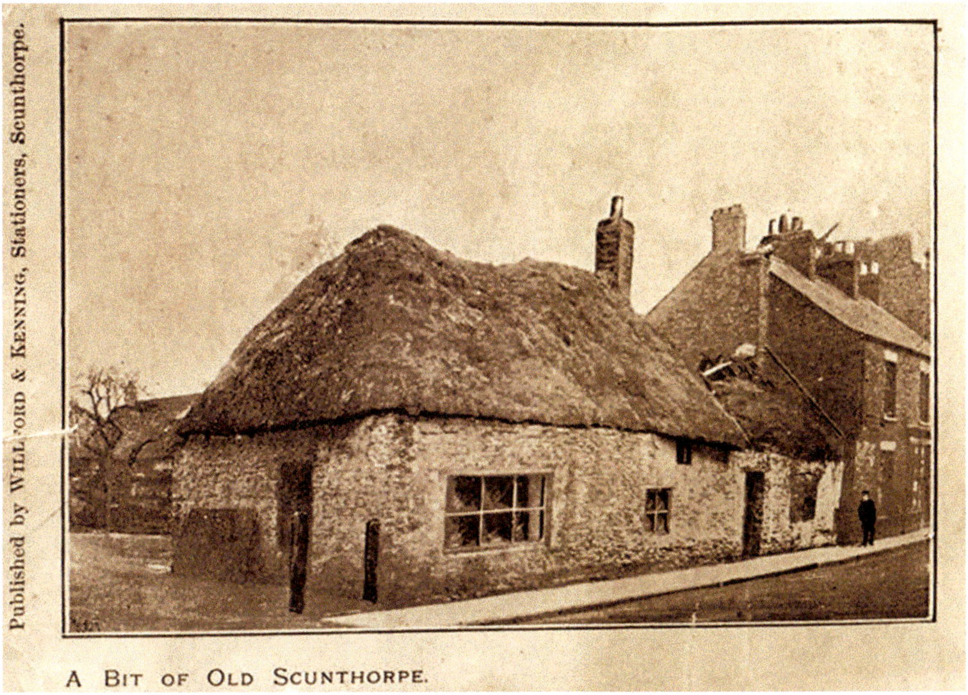

'A bit of old Scunthorpe'.

The boom in steel production had taken the entire industry within Britain by surprise, but this newfound stability allowed a greater degree of economic planning and business confidence within the area. Business enterprise estates or industrial parks built near to the steelworks in Flixborough (and nearly every township of Scunthorpe) had either sprung up or set their development to work, and began to recruit staff to fulfil their operations from then on. It is most likely from this point forward that Scunthorpe partook a mission of industrial diversity that came away somewhat, but not entirely, from the steel industry. While it is obvious that the steelworks is one of the town's biggest employers, the ability and success of these new businesses came from this surge in population. Scunthorpe is home to a wide array of markets – from leisure to retail – and has come a long way from its uncertain beginnings to the firm constitution it has now been for some time.

DID YOU KNOW?

The water supply in Flixborough played a key role in the village's existence. The Saxons were lucky to have such an accessible source, which may help explain the status of those who once resided in the area. The village was also relatively predominant in textile manufacture according to sources, an element of its independence during the period.

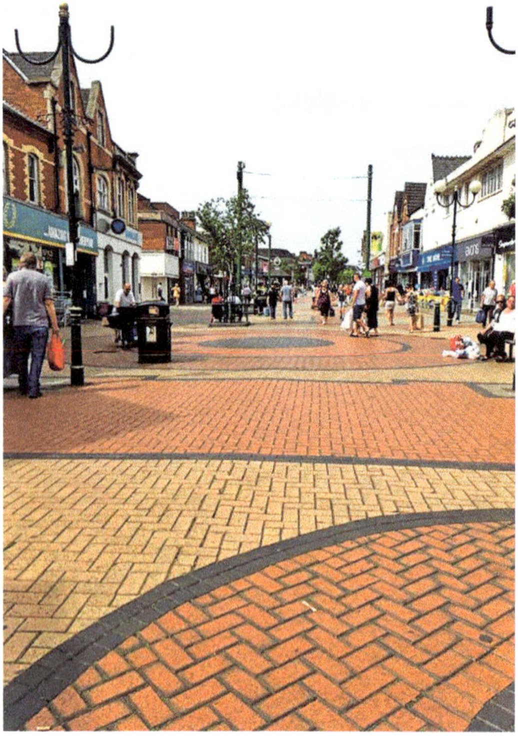

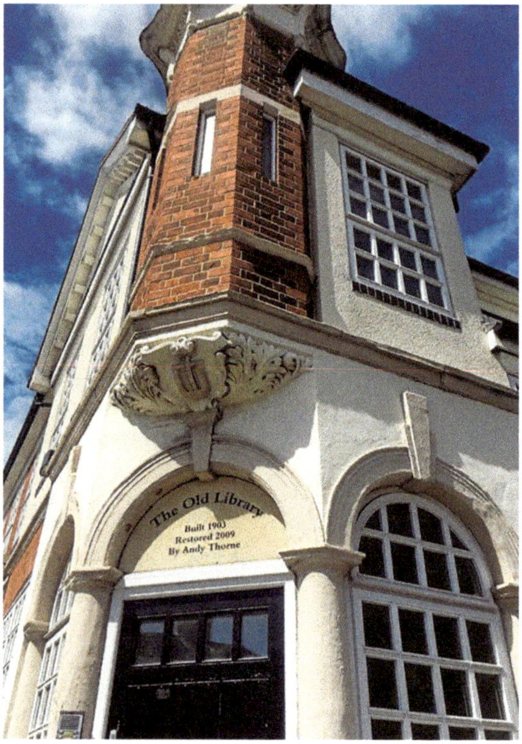

Above left: The busy High Street of modern Scunthorpe.

Above right: The library was built to provide for a new neighbourhood.

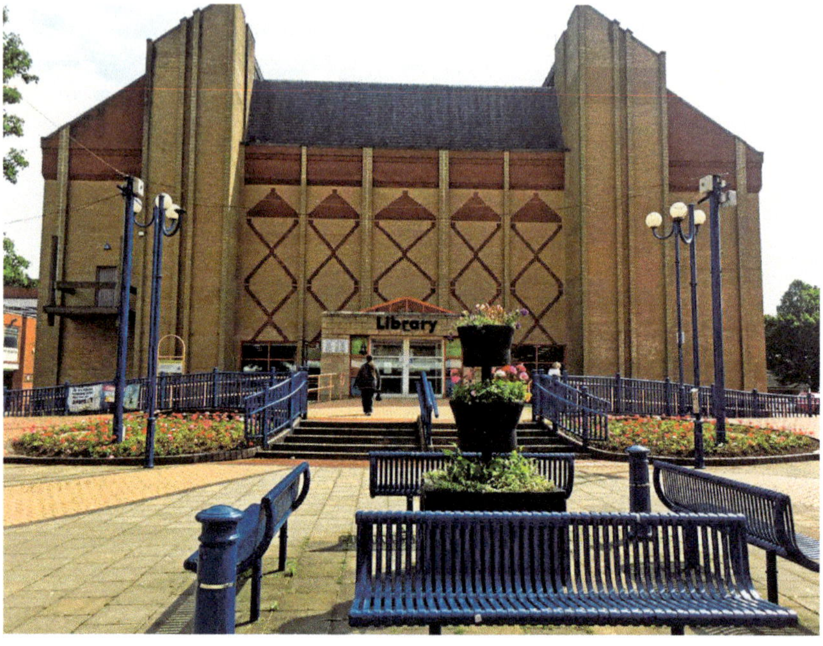

The library today was built in the town centre.

3. The Steel Industry, Railways and Manufacture

For anyone who is unfamiliar with the town of Scunthorpe, one of the first things you are likely to learn is that the steel industry is found everywhere within the town. Scunthorpe, however, is not entirely a town wedged between the huge masses of metal, but is rather a place where the production of steel is celebrated in many different ways. The steelworks are indeed of great size: even from the motorway entrances the works are often visible on the horizon, whether that be the structures themselves or just the smoke coming from them. But even if you don't happen to view the site, or perchance even visit the Scunthorpe itself, the town's football club demonstrates the importance and dedication to the legacy of the steel industry.

When planning the structure of this book, I shared a simultaneous desire to make the steel section a large proportion of it, in correspondence with its role in the town, but also for it to not overshadow the other lesser-known aspects of Scunthorpe. It is quite often that we find Scunthorpe is judged by the presence of the steel industry, whether this comes from people inside or outside of the town. This connotation is indeed mostly negative: people associate an industrial town with dirtiness and uncleanliness, but the

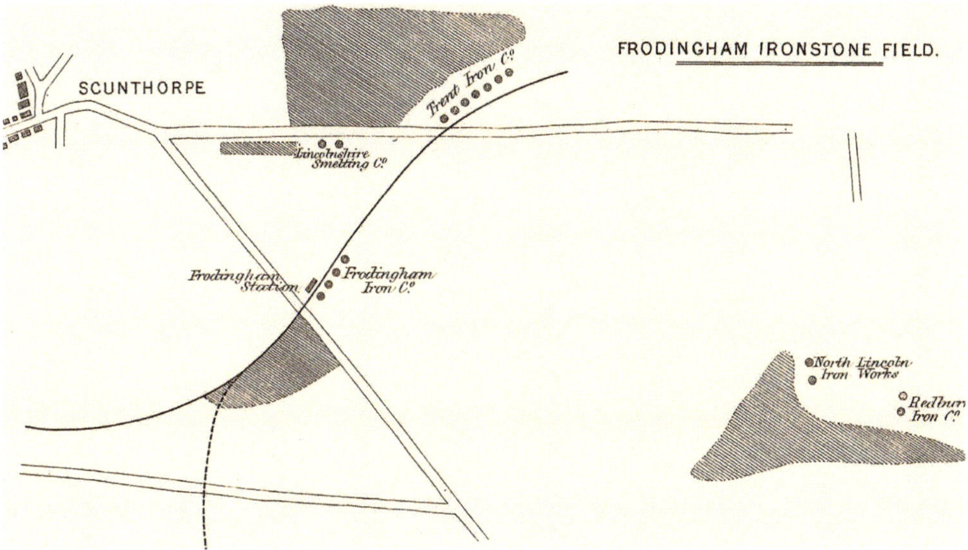

A basic map showing Scunthorpe's mineral land and railway lines.

truth is that the majority of the town is not this way and it is difficult for anywhere industrial to look incredibly attractive. But what is important, or rather ironic, is that less and less of us know the history of the great works. This is not because of a lack of interest or the shortness of available information, but perhaps because when we grow up with this place existing in our town it becomes a symbol of home rather than an interest to explore. Nearly everyone within Scunthorpe will either work themselves, have a family member, or have friends who work within the town's steel industry due to the massive influence and employment of the site. Despite its influence on Scunthorpe, I feel it is quite easy to forget or overlook its significance when its presence has become very 'normal' to our everyday lives. From the working conditions to the hours required to run an entire production of steel, the industry of Scunthorpe deserves to have its history shared.

It was first thought that Rowland Winn discovered the iron ore within Lindsey that formed the start of Scunthorpe's steel industry, and that in some respects this may be seen as the birth of the steel industry within the North Lincolnshire region. However, it is understood that during the Roman period some settlers near to Appleby had previously discovered the rich iron deposits. It is not clear what – or if – these settlers had intended to use their new findings, but it appears that Winn actually rediscovered the previously concealed ore. While living in Appleby Hall, Winn allegedly knew of the Roman settlement around the areas of Scunthorpe. Due to their handiwork in creating metal objects such as household items and defensive protection, it is possible that he believed that the chances of finding more of these reserves were likely. There are many stories on how the iron ore was rediscovered by Rowland Winn, which is likely because some people were unaware of previous settlements in the area. Some sources claim that the discovery actually came as a surprise while roadbuilding was taking place, and that during the digging process the ore happened to be found in the ground in the particular area the roads were set to be built. After archaeological excavations, it seemed more probable that the Romans had settled because of the deposits, meaning that Winn and possibly others were able to take a favourable gamble on the likelihood of a new business to be made.

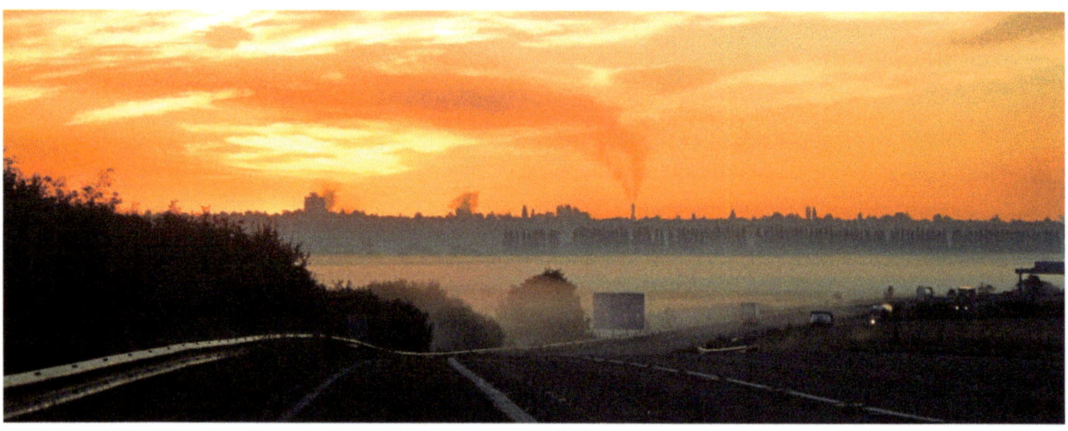

'The Heavens Reflect Our Labours'.[2]

When the ore was discovered, it is often mentioned that fears brewed over the new town becoming the 'second Middlesbrough' in regard to its level of potential industrial output. The truth is rather that the ore had to be first tested in order to conclude if the metal was worthy enough to be set into production, and therefore prove a profitable business to invest in. Due to the initially poor samples collected and the seemingly meagre quality of the ore, it was doubtful that the discovery would ever turn out well. It was a surprise for Winn himself when it was found that the iron reserves were rich and of good quality. The land around Scunthorpe was allegedly easy to mine, and made the entire process much easier for success to be made. The ironworks developed from around 1875 after it was decided the ore could bloom into a successful industry. It is interesting to question whether the industry today is what Winn would ever have anticipated from his first discovery.

Initially, the iron production began near to Barnsley and Rotherham in South Yorkshire, where the ironstone resources were transported and tested by the Dawes in order to create the beginning of a manufactured product. Transporting the ore was initially carried out by a horse and carriage carrying a hefty load over the boarder of Lincolnshire into Yorkshire, which was obviously at the time a long and dull process but also the only route of transportation. Over time, however, the local railways surrounding the settlement were constructed and allowed entrepreneurs to obtain the necessary materials to form the basis of iron production within Scunthorpe.

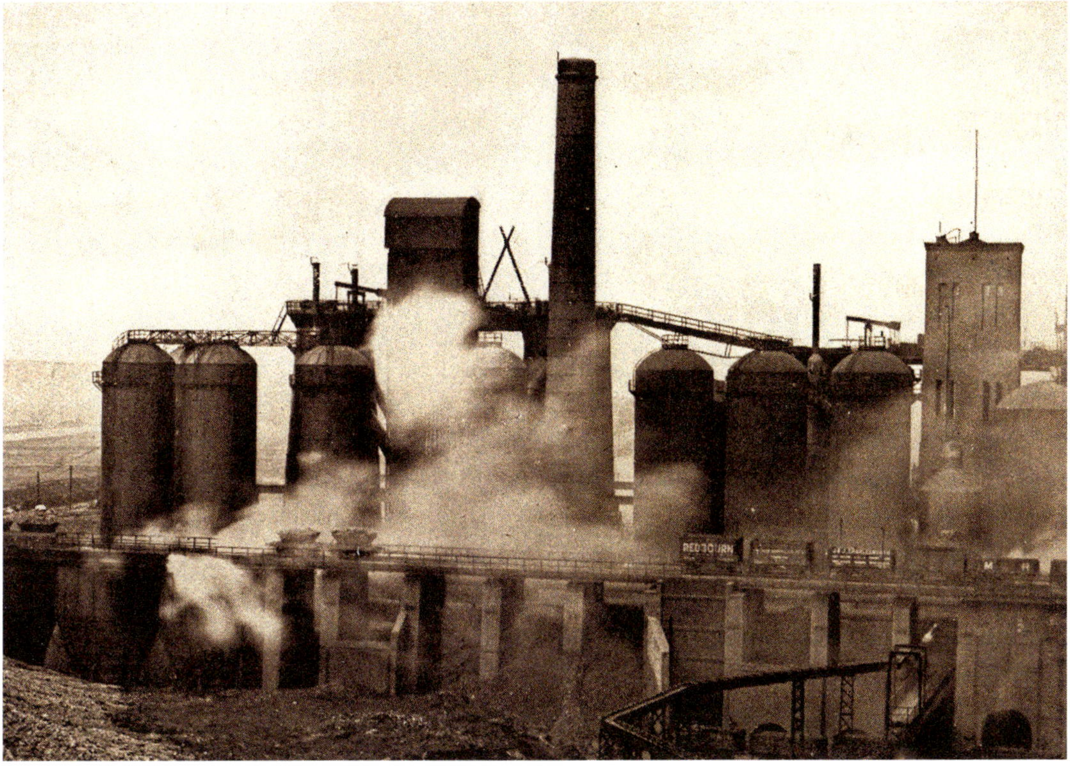

The Redbourn Hill ironworks in full swing, 1918.

The process of setting up an entire industry within such an open landscape was not as easy a task as you would expect, in comparison with a large city or suburban area for example. Hurdles such as leases and agreements constantly presented themselves, and just as one was over it was not long before a new wave of issues became apparent. Blast furnaces began to be constructed in the villages surrounding Scunthorpe such as Appleby, and iron ore mines, steel mills and quarries were put in place and dug out to supply the newly found treasure to be processed. Coal or coke was imported to the port of Immingham, making the Grimsby and other North Lincolnshire railways (the Axholme and Trent) so significant to the production process. It is reported that Rowland Winn was responsible for promoting railway links with Sir Berkley Sheffield in the 1860s, making the railway system much more effective during the start of Scunthorpe's initial industry.

DID YOU KNOW?

The four current blast furnaces at the Scunthorpe Steelworks are named after four queens. Anne, Bess, Victoria and Mary stand proudly as the iconic image of Scunthorpe.

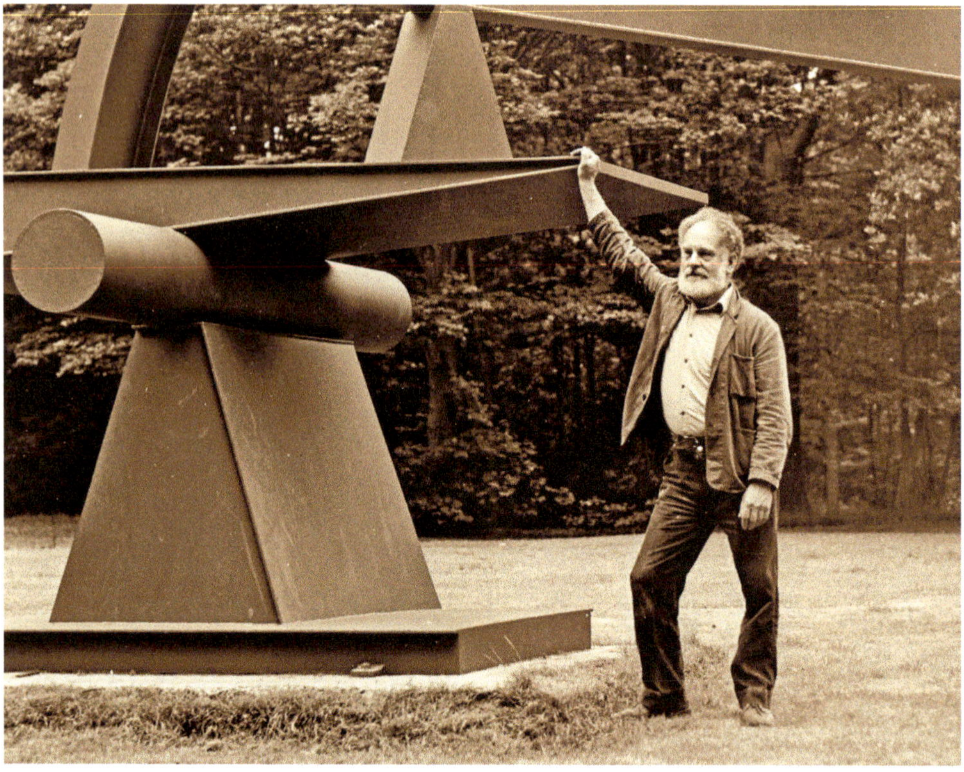

Sculptor Roy Kitchin at the Appleby-Froddingham works.

The industries of Appleby-Frodingham, Redbourn Ironworks and Normanby Works all set up sites to begin the production of iron on a sizable scale. Once these sites were set up, a number of different works appeared alongside the initial steelworks. The North Lincolnshire and Trent Ironworks became part of the Appleby-Frodingham Steel Co. in 1934 as a way to increase the productive capacity. This is also why many establishments such as local football clubs are known as 'app-frodd' for short after the steelworks. While they began as separate plants, they came to form a nationalised trade in the late 1960s as the British Steel Corporation. This was likely part of the decision in 1967 to nationalise at least ninety per cent of the steel industry, and now forms part of the steel's story of ownership. Just before the year 2000 the British Steel Corporation (BSC) became part of the Corus Group as a nationalised firm, which occurred when BSC merged with a Dutch company. Part of this project aimed to increase productivity by increasing the amount of investment into the industry, hoping that the quantity of produce as well as the workplace efficiency would rise. Later, the Scunthorpe Steelworks owned by Corus would be taken over by Tata Steel for a short period, before finally becoming owned up to the present period by Greybull Capital, part of British Steel Ltd.

As the steel industry grew bigger and its productive capabilities expanded, the demand for its produce grew during the First and Second World Wars. The industry did well to bounce back after many plants closed during the Great Depression in the late 1920

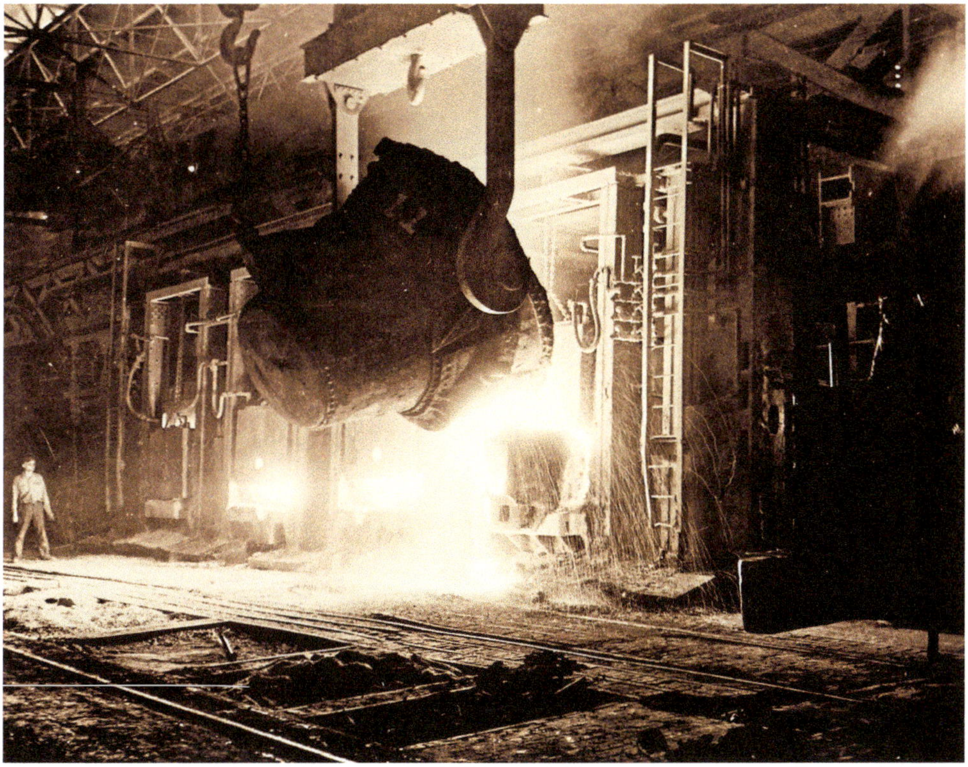

Pig iron such as this became part of Scunthorpe's reputation.

and 1930s, including some of Scunthorpe's central ironworks. The iron manufacture was converted to the production of steel in order to efficiently supply a ready-made commodity that did not require much further processing. Mines had remained open since the industry had been set up despite the economical setbacks, and required more labour to work the land. More workers were recruited and production became increasingly intense in order to cope with the pressure. Though this had occurred earlier, when the industry first became known as a functioning entity, the fluidity from agricultural work to quarry and steel labouring became especially useful. But this was no task for plucking people from farming and making them work in a pit; instead the demand for work could only be met by an influx of labourers and longer working hours. As men were required to fight for the country at war, the number of workers drained from the steel industry and made the output deficit larger and larger to fill.

During the Second World War in particular, women were recruited to labour at the steelworks to help ease the tense demand for output, perhaps serving one of the greatest opportunities to provide skills and training. Though some women who were employed during the period tell of simply being assigned to cleaning duties, it is known that women actually worked their way around the factory and fulfilled the roles they desired. Locomotive work was one of the areas women worked when the carriages would arrive at the plant. As the war dragged on, women would increasingly make up a significant percentage of the labour force. It is thanks to these women that the steel industry – not just in Scunthorpe, but all around the United Kingdom – was able to successfully produce the amount of output needed despite the intense working environment.

From the outside, it is believed that the entire industry simply operates, but unfortunately there have been a number of fatalities at the plant since its opening. All of these accidents have been due to mishaps, and some down to explosions in the high-risk environment; one instance of an explosion that occurred in 1975 demonstrates how sensitive the industry is. It is also worth bearing in mind that others have suffered life-changing injuries during their time at the plant. Today a memorial stands for those who have tragically lost their lives at the steelworks, based near the fountain and facing the town centre.

It is important to remember when we consider the history, when you look at those blast furnaces or talk to anyone who works at the steelworks it becomes clear that setting it up to become what it is today was never going to be an easy or smooth process. And even after it was set up, its maintenance and survival is still the most critical situation of its existence.

There have been many times since the opening of the steel industry that changes of ownership and job losses have become a particularly relevant issue. At the last instance of a change in ownership, campaigns such as 'save our steel' came about within the town.

The campaign against job losses has struck a chord in recent years with many in the town. This is most likely due to the fact that it is quite frequent job losses are set to take place every couple of years, with the amount that are employed by the industry it is unsurprising that so many are effected. Other campaigns such as those in Redcar became famous locally. With the importance of preserving valued industries within Britain, it is very easy to see how a whole community can quickly unite over a common interest.

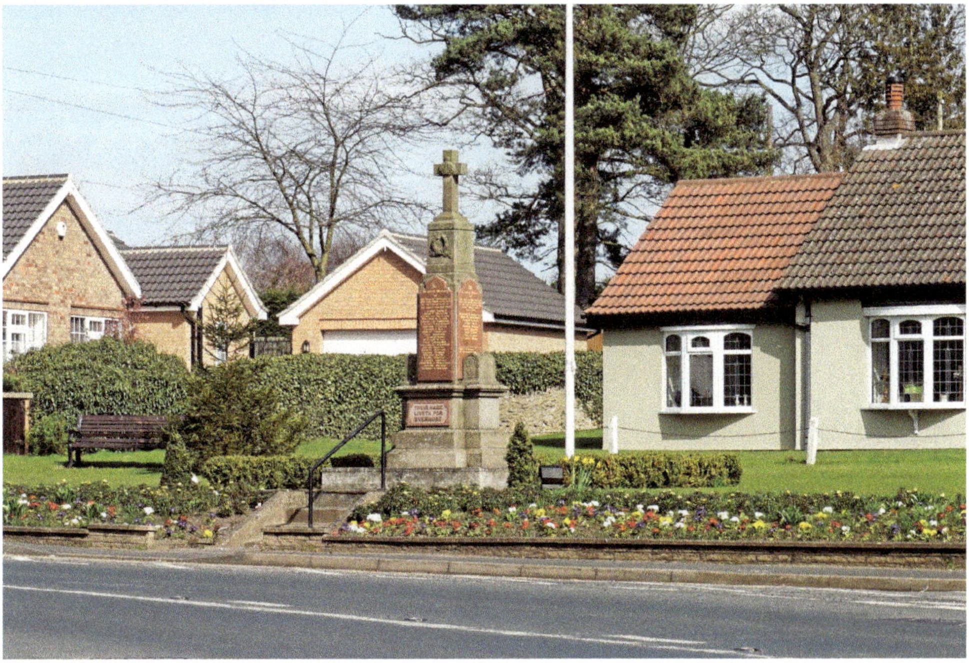

A war memorial dedicated in memory. (Courtesy of Ian S.)

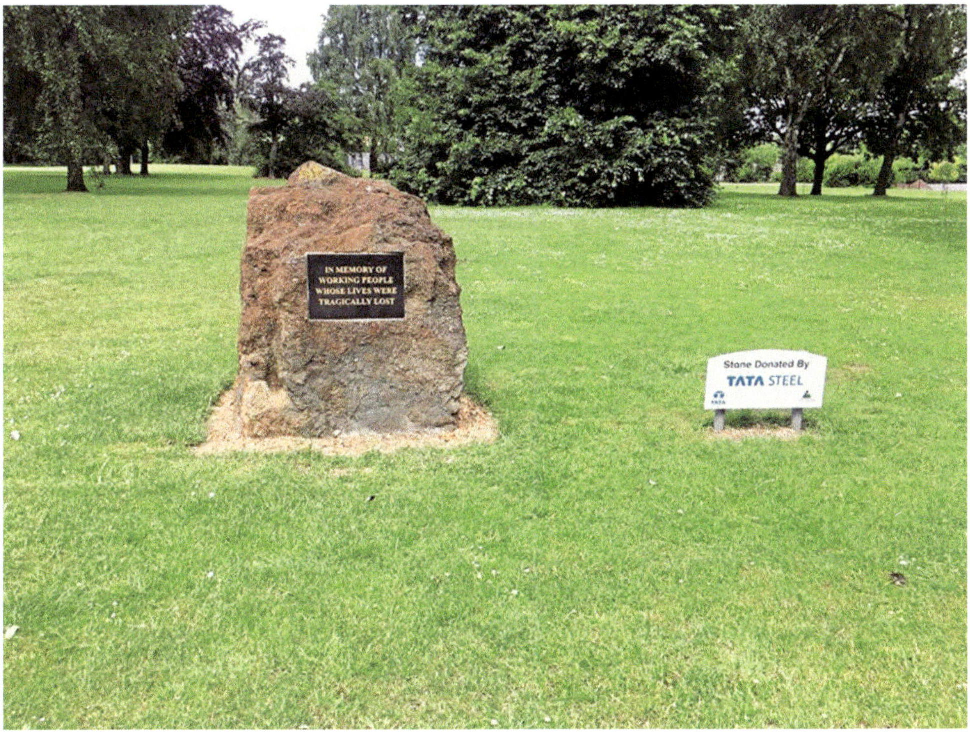

In memory of those workers who died fighting. (Courtesy of Dave Wright)

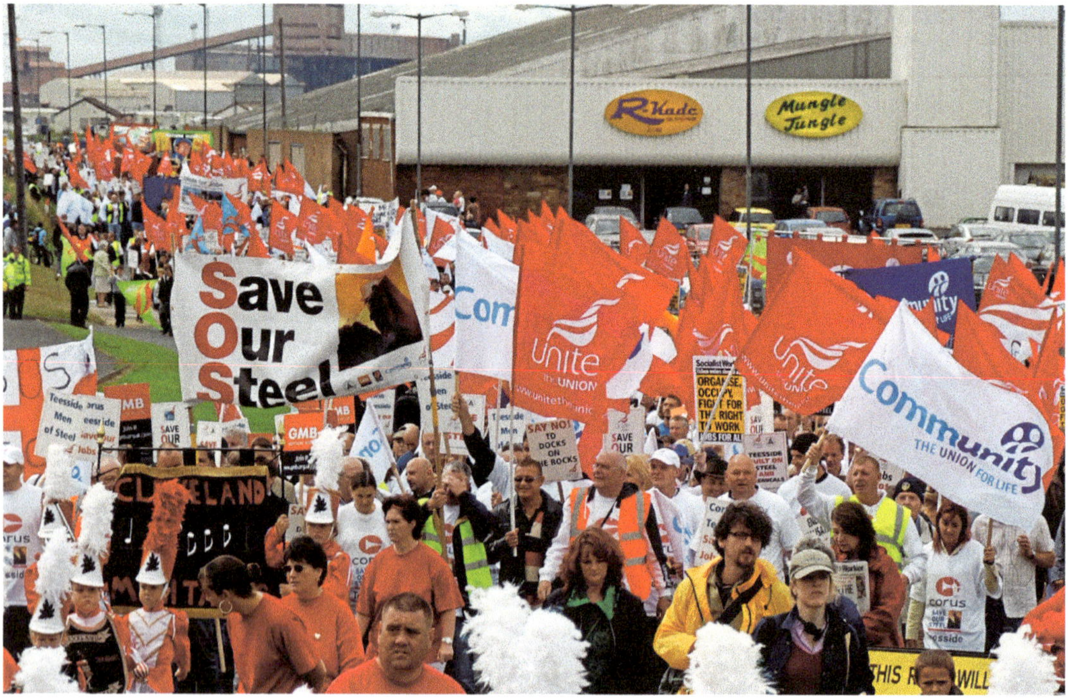

Protesters marching in Redcar, similar to Scunthorpe. (Courtesy of David Aisbett)

Railways: An Extension of Scunthorpe Steel

To have a town successfully producing steel is one thing, but to transport this produce into the place it is demanded is another. Soon after the general establishment that the ironstone under the care of Rowland Winn would be put to industrial usage, the rail links to Scunthorpe and its villages began to develop massively so the processed steel could be shipped efficiently. The railways of Scunthorpe are both a fundamental and vital element of Scunthorpe steel and its success. Today we often use the transport link to travel to Cleethorpes or Manchester, but the importance of those same railways remain.

The first train station at Scunthorpe was constructed in the 1880s during the gradual increase in activity and population within the local area. The primary purpose of this first station was to transport passengers to local villages as the steel network's boom followed relatively soon after. Once this went out of use due to renovation, the new station that stands today was built in 1928.

DID YOU KNOW?

Scunthorpe's old station was actually called Frodingham station before the new one was built. This was quite clearly due to the town not being formed, and Frodingham having its own station because of its proximity both to the steelworks and the majority of the town's population.

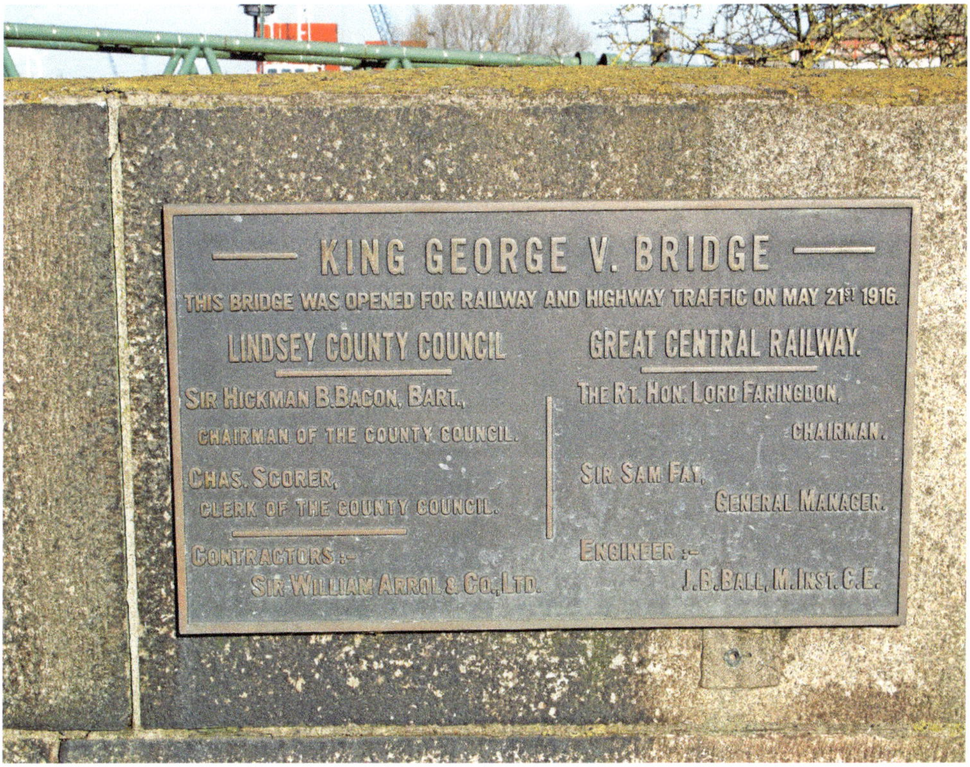

The plaque of the walkway over the bridge. (Courtesy of Angus@townley.com)

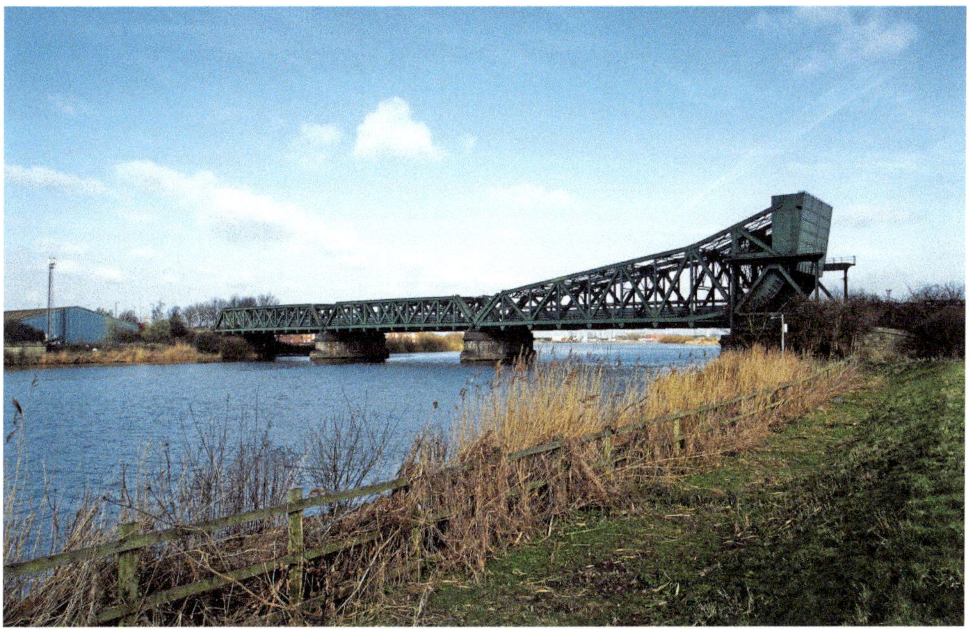

The King George V Bridge at Keadby. (Courtesy of Angus@townley.com)

Trains running towards the west of the town from Doncaster, Sheffield and Manchester run over the eighty-five-arch viaduct, which continues towards the King George V bridge. This viaduct can be seen from Scotter Road and cars have run underneath it since it was constructed. In 1911, the viaduct was partly filled up in order to form an embankment structure along large parts of the railway. There have been multiple reasons as to why the embankment was constructed: many believe it is safer for trains in an emergency, while people have been known to enjoy the grass that has grown on the land since.

Another railway station, known as Dawes Lane, was also in use shortly before the new Scunthorpe-Frodingham station was rebuilt. Though it only functioned on a small village route, it is said to have been popular when it was first opened, though the majority of the lines unfortunately closed soon after the main station was in full swing.

Around Scunthorpe a number of unemployed signal boxes exist that are often stationed at the beginning of a wold. These signal boxes are in fact based all over England and have remained out of use because of the development of new technology for railroad crossings, but are still protected often as at least Grade II-listed buildings. While it is rather unusual to see them frequently (unless you live in a village) many are open to observation for those interested – however it is not advisable to venture inside. The first one I encountered while doing fieldwork out at Gainsthorpe was the Kirton Lime Sidings, located just near the end of the small village.

This signal box was created as part of the Manchester, Sheffield and Lincolnshire railway system. Other signal boxes in a relatively close distance include those at Appleby and Elsham, which also happen to be part of this same network. After the creation of this

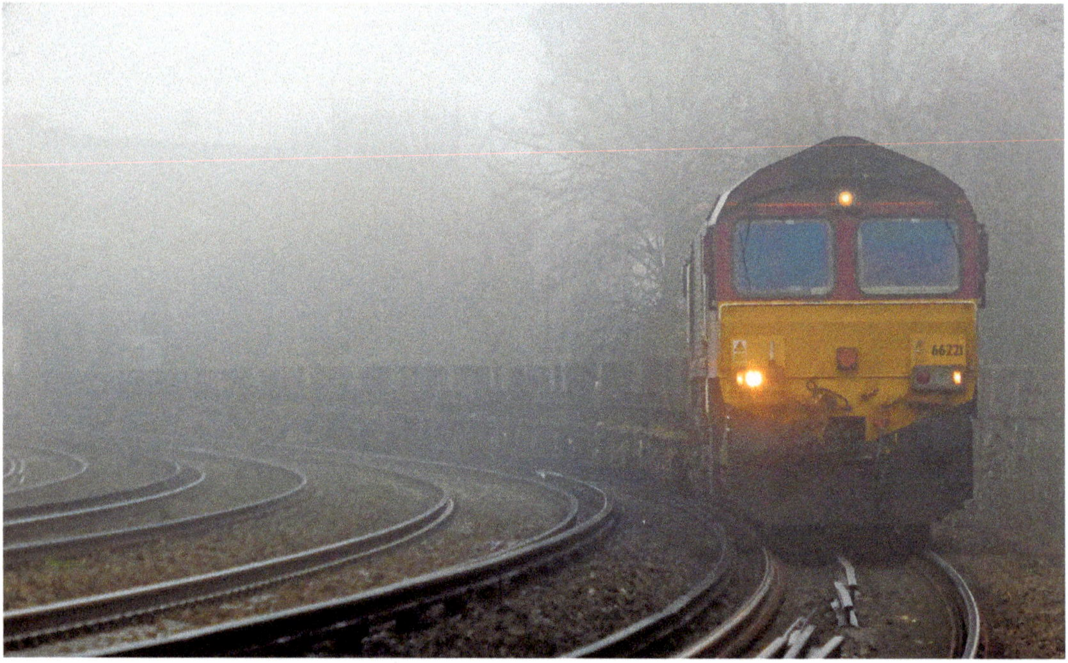

An empty steel train on the Scunthorpe line.

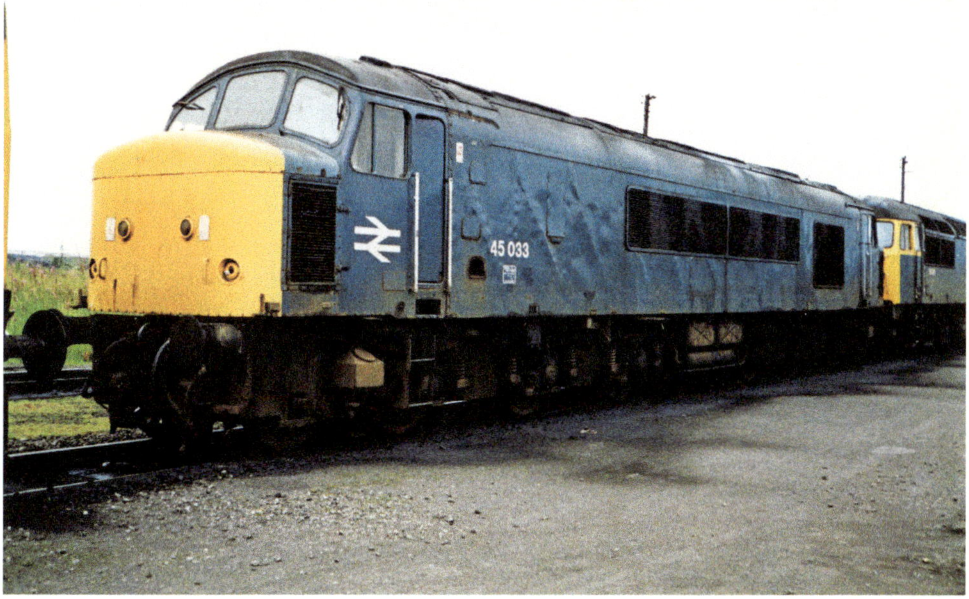

Above: The trains run through here, but very irregularly.

Right: The trains run on top of the viaduct towards Doncaster.

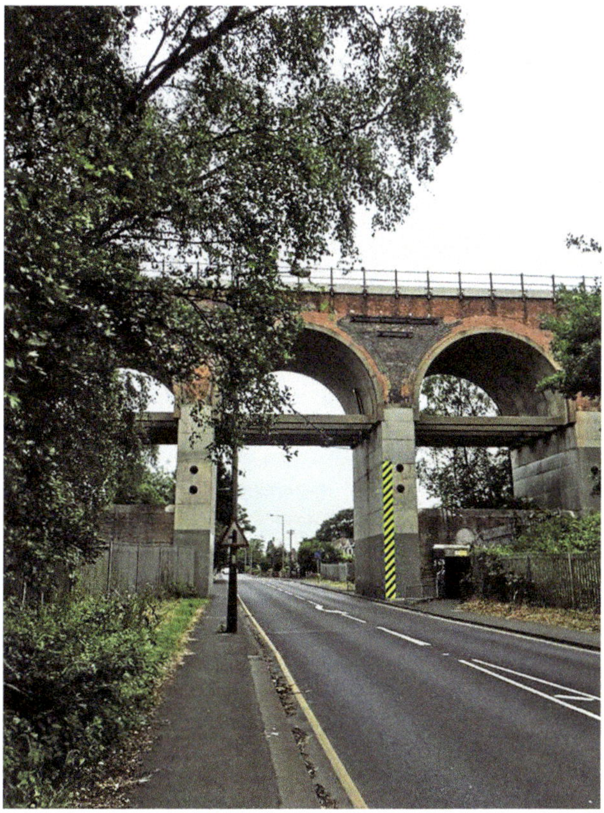

railway network, it later became known as the Great Central Railway and came to include another signal boxed located at Wrawby and Brocklesby Junction.

The steelworks at Scunthorpe does actually have its own functioning network of railways that operates entirely within the boundaries of the plant. This is quite clearly used to transport manufactured steel around the works and then is hauled off to its destination. Quite often, if you are passing by the outskirts of the industry, you are able to see the cargo trains moving around the plant. Today, the Appleby-Frodingham Railways Preservation Society offers trips that take passengers around parts of the steelworks. While the society owns its own locomotives, the majority of these are fully functioning and are used to give riders an insight as to what goes on inside the gates of steel production. The reason for the existence of this society is because events would take place in celebration of the steelworks that would involve the public in the town's legacy. While locomotives would take interested onlookers on a tour, the events became more popular as the years went on and, consequently, the preservation society was born to fulfil this same role.

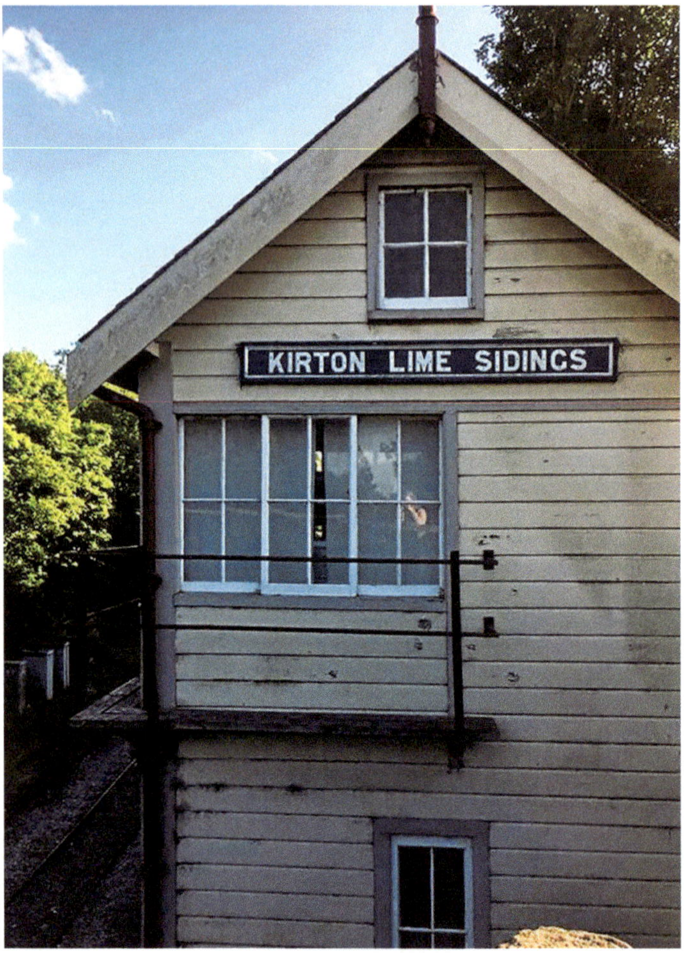

Another Grade II-listed building out of use.

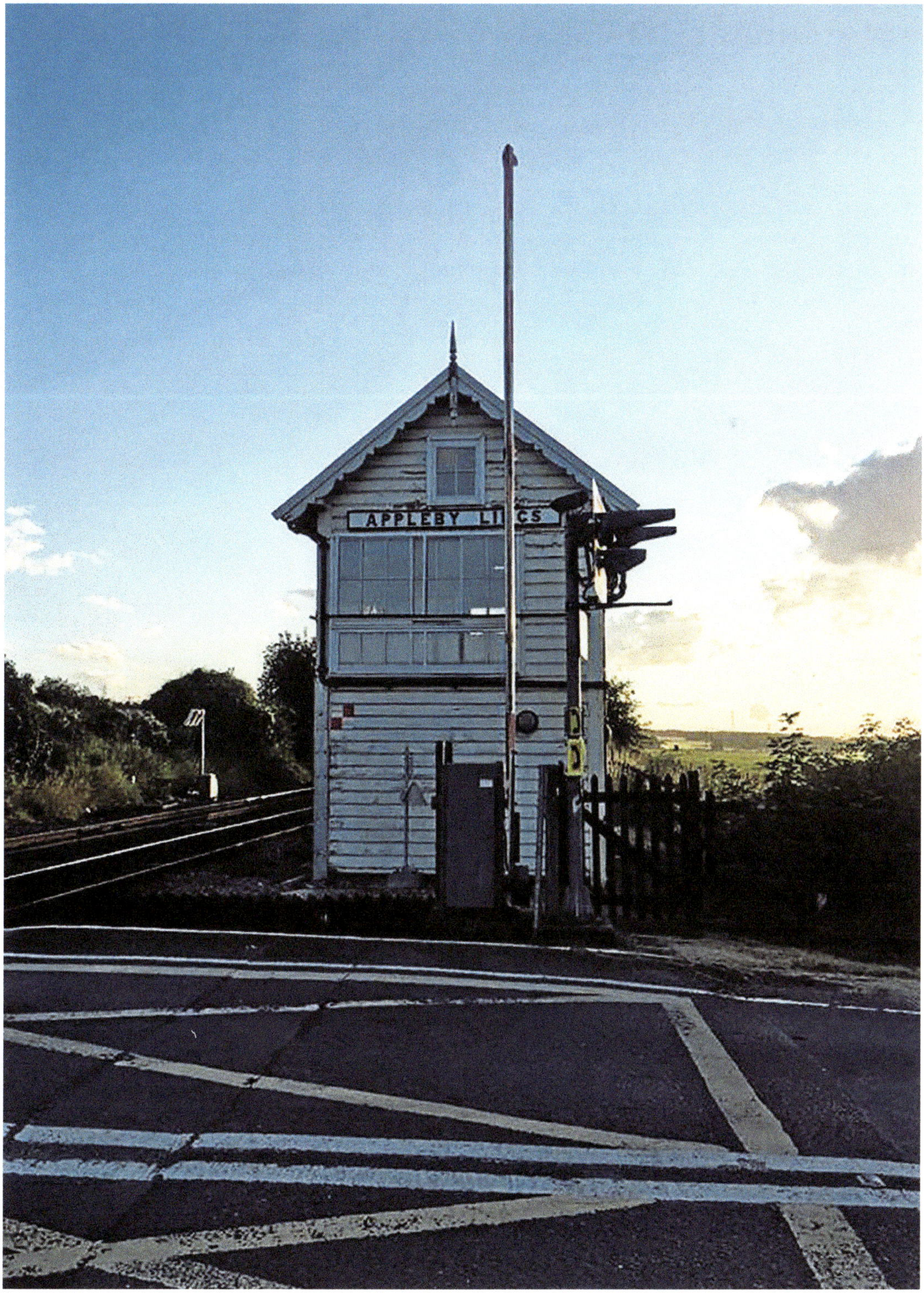

Appleby's signal box.

The railways of Scunthorpe may not seem particularly interesting to many, but it should always be emphasised that the transportation to and from the town would be made much more difficult without it – both for steel and passengers. The setup of the railways both within the steelworks and those adjoining to access beyond the town are fundamental to the existence of the steelworks today. Though transport was previously carried out by man and horse, it is safe to say that rail has made the journey of Scunthorpe's steel production. Although steel was never going to be an uphill success, it is not without the effort of the owners, the railways and most importantly the relentless labour of the steelworkers that have allowed Scunthorpe and its steel to survive.

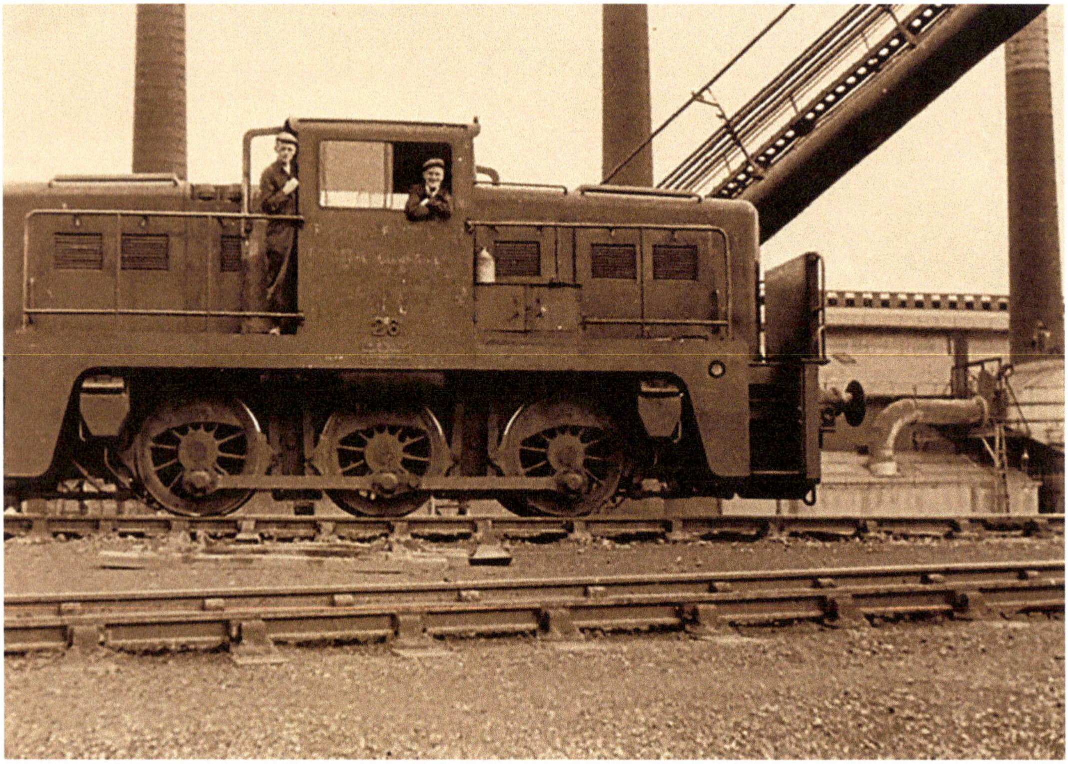

One of the first trains at Appleby.

4. An Industrial Garden Town: A Celebration of Its Gardens

Scunthorpe has, in some respects, built up a reputation for its status as an industrial garden town. Its title is proudly displayed on each signpost welcoming you into the town, but this is often one of the only ways people are made aware of its prestige. In some respects, it perhaps demonstrates the most significance of its title when the concepts of 'industrial' and 'gardens' are both brought to light to compare their contrasting yet purposeful existence. I feel that there is a large stigma around my hometown, and it's one that I would rather like to challenge, or at least attempt to do so. I think many people believe that Scunthorpe and other industrialised places are 'unattractive', but while some areas are not as pretty as we may want them at be, it is true that most towns will have areas that are similar. The gardens of Scunthorpe are not given the full amount of appreciation they deserve, though we are quick to enjoy them during the hot weather. It goes without saying, therefore, that the work provided by the North Lincolnshire Council is – year on year – a phenomenal contribution that allows not only the visual upkeep but the deserving title Scunthorpe proudly holds.

Every year open gardens take place all over the town and in the surrounding Wolds in support of Lindsey Lodge Hospice. These competitions allow others to spectate and enjoy the work others put into their gardens and often result in welcoming others into your own premises. While open gardens occur almost everywhere and are indeed not open spaces for the entire public to enjoy, it does present the opportunity to discuss the question of why we have gardens. We have our own gardens because we are attracted to them aesthetically and we feel a reward when they appear presentable. If we consider this on a larger scale, it becomes apparent that public gardens mix together the feeling of pleasure and relaxation; our open spaces are much more than a landscape filler.

Festival Gardens

Scunthorpe opened some of its gardens in celebration of the Festival Gardens season, part of the Festival of Britain. The festival focused on rejoicing the achievements of Britain after the Second World War under a Labour government who wanted to encourage an integrated and united society recovering from the outcome of war. Though the Festival of Britain was mainly based on the Southbank of London, it was also heavily featured in larger cities such as York. Scunthorpe, as well as many other smaller areas, also celebrated this event, which is likely to have been due to the united effort in steel production and the overall success of the industry. The main park to be opened and enjoyed during the festival was Central Park, arguably the most famous park within Scunthorpe for this very reason. From the Civic Centre entrance to the park, the open gardens are named as Queens Gardens at the north and south locations, demonstrating the significance of national royal celebrations inclusive of Scunthorpe.

Central Park

Everyone who lives in Scunthorpe will know Central Park. This park, situated towards the centre of town, accommodates everyone and includes cycle and walking lanes, a car park, benches, a playground, the Splashpad for summer weather and a small shop. The most significant (or indeed the most famous) aspect of Central Park is the fountain situated in the centre of the gardens.

The greenery and benches make the park and fountain a popular choice for a trip out, and is particularly popular with dog walkers and those wishing to keep active as a result of the flatter landscape. The park is located next door to the Civic Centre (Scunthorpe's council offices) and The Pods leisure centre. Central Park is also home to Scunthorpe's parkrun on a Saturday morning, in which many locals attend to complete the circuit run.

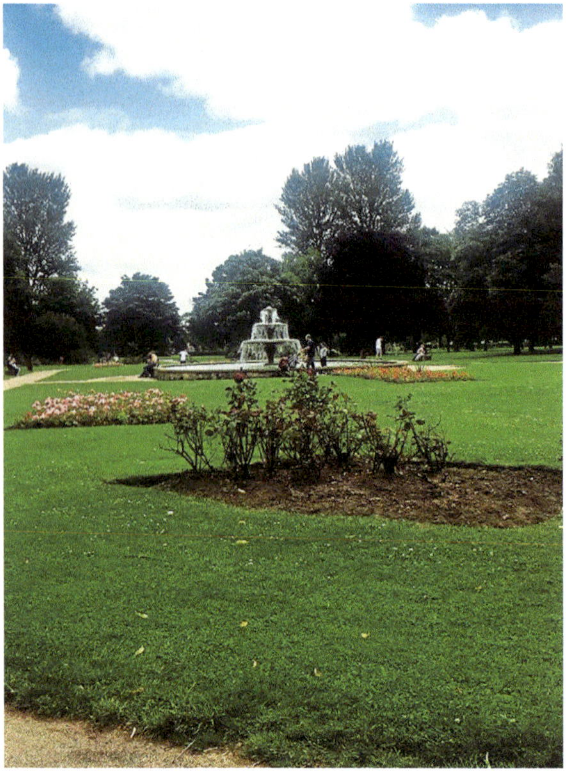

The Central Park fountain. (Courtesy of Peter Woodward)

Kingsway Gardens

Kingsway Gardens offers a large open space on the west side of town, near the Berkley Circle roundabout. The eco-friendly gardens feature an array of flower beds from early spring to late autumn, a more secluded and relaxed environment. Wildlife is allowed to flourish in the gardens, with wildlife boxes and careful housekeeping employed here. The park does feature a small children's playground towards its exit, with a hill and flagpole at the east of the park offering a view of the entire gardens.

The park can be seen as a sloped landscape with large floral displays, featuring a roundabout-themed presentation near the road entrance. The background of the park at its highest point includes the Skippingdale housing and industrial estate, and faces towards the villages of Gunness and Keadby.

Kingsway Gardens was awarded the Green Flag Award in 2016. This has been awarded for the ninth time successively, acknowledging not only the efforts of the gardening team and the high quality of their work but the contribution to the town's reputation and pride. This award recognises hard work and dedication to open spaces and parks for the community to enjoy, and is an example of the persistent devotion the management of Kingsway Gardens has in ensuring there is a space that accommodates everyone.

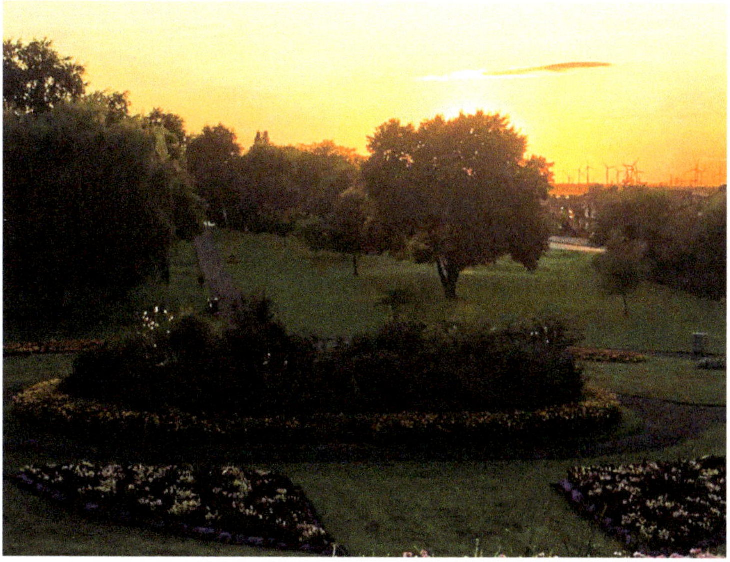

Kingsway Gardens in the evening capturing the town's skyline.

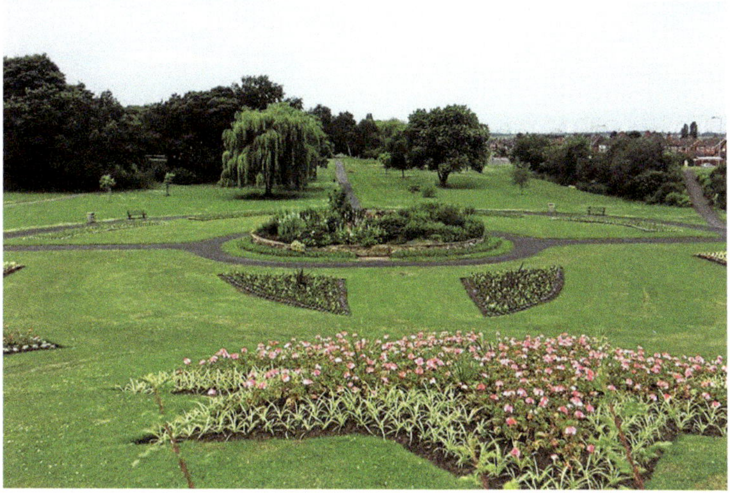

Taken from the top of the garden hill.

Normanby Hall

Although not strictly within the town, Normanby Hall is branded as belonging to the Scunthorpe's outer Wolds and districts, such as the small village of Normanby. Located just before Barton-upon-Stather, the estate is a popular venue for weddings and other related events such as proms and formal events.

The hall had servants that would tend to the residents' needs and often prepare their food, so it is not difficult to imagine the size and wealth of the estate.

DID YOU KNOW?

The servants in Normanby Hall were built their own wing to live and take rest in while they served there. It was of a large size and was built by Walter Brierley, but unfortunately was not in place for much longer than fifty years as it was demolished in 1949.

The stable (often known as the courtyard area today) was designed by Robert Smirke during the early nineteenth century, estimated around the year 1820. The hall often sported gardeners who played an important role in its running due to the large size of the estate and its acres of garden area. The head gardener, in fact, would have lived in the village of Normanby due to the ease accessibility to the premises, which would have perhaps been relevant as vandalism and theft was a huge concern for the property. During the First World War, Normanby Hall became a voluntary aid detachment hospital to supply extra resources and space for casualties and preparation.

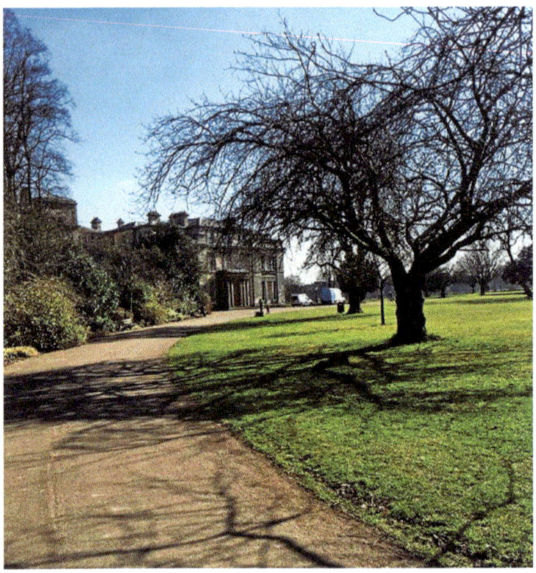

The hall at the end of the car and footpath.

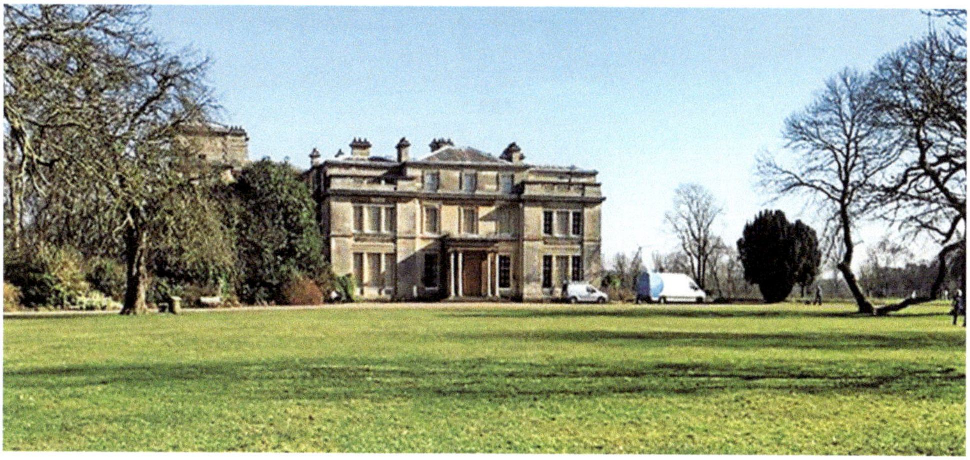

Another take on the hall and its gardens.

Normanby Hall offers a large display of gardens and forest to its visitors, as well as a small animal sanctuary that often features deer, duck ponds, a playground and miniature railway, Victorian walled gardens, a gift shop, café, an information desk and a farming museum. The park itself is named after the hall, and was constructed over the years 1825–30 to the designs of Robert Smirke for Sir Robert Sheffield. The Sheffield family had been residing at the estate since 1539, not moving out of Normanby Hall until 1963. Today the hall has now become a part of Scunthorpe Borough Council, allowing visitors to enjoy the grounds and engage with its history due to it being leased to the council a year after the family moved out. Part of this includes the gallery within Normanby Hall that can be viewed on certain days, along with the museum in the courtyard.

In addition to this, Normanby Hall is the venue for many other events too due to its large site and degree of accessibility. Some of these have come to include classic car shows, camping at certain times during the year, and the annual Race for Life.

While Central Park, Kingsway Gardens and Normanby Hall are the main gardens within Scunthorpe's boundaries, there are indeed other areas of preserved land and beauty that deserve some degree of recognition. While these may not fit the idea of 'gardens' as such, it is important to note that these areas are enjoyed by the community of Scunthorpe in a similar way that the parks are. After Scunthorpe became formed from its five townships, it became possible to have designated spaces preserved for the purpose of enjoyment and leisure. When people picture what an industrial town looks like, it is not surprising that many would depict a bleak or polluted landscape. The fact is that towns like Scunthorpe do not wholly match this image, and the gardens and preserved areas are what will enable this stereotype to be rethought.

Ashby Ville Nature Reserve

Often known for its large lake and accompanying trail, Ashby Ville is located across from the steelworks at the edge of Scunthorpe. The nature reserve is home to many forms of wildlife and features a bridge, sandbanks, and an ideal place for rambling. Jet skiers are a typical sight in the warmer months from late spring to autumn.

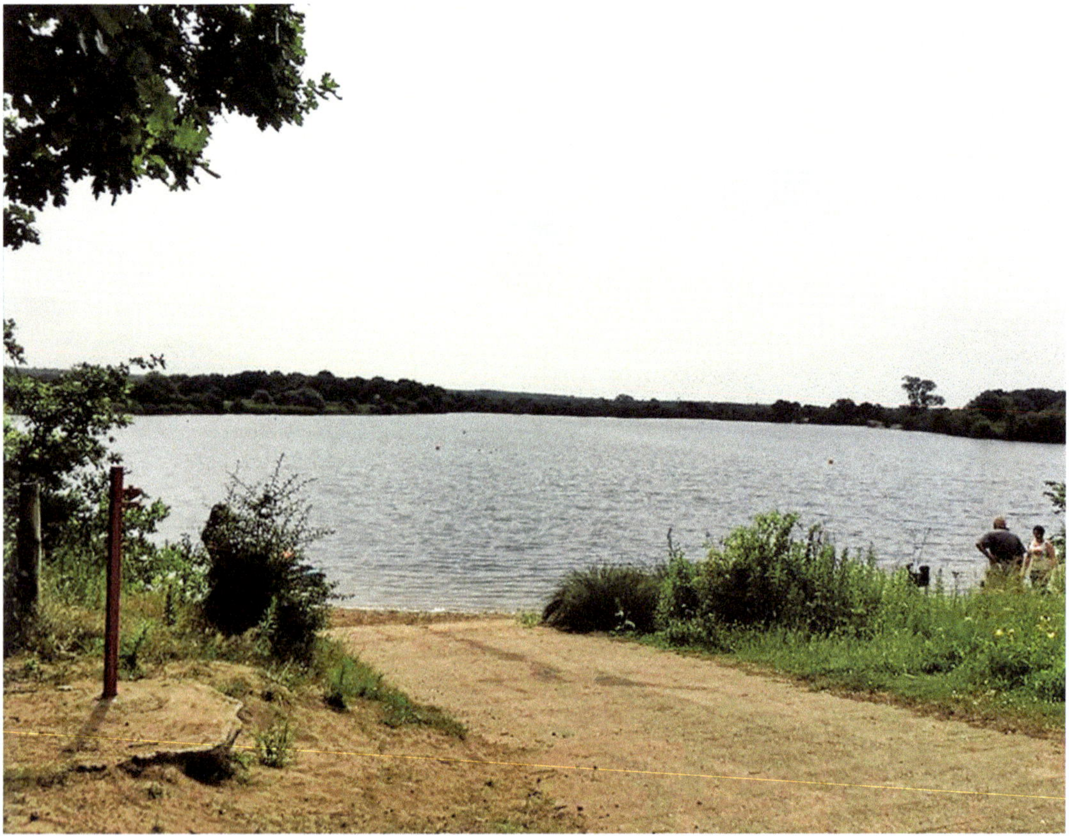

Taken from the steelworks entrance of the site.

The majority of the lake's jet-ski and water events have an access area located by the steelworks' entrance. At the opposite side of the lake lies another entrance with a larger car park that is best suited for dog walking. The nature reserve is situated in an ideal location next to a small shopping centre and a supermarket, making it very accessible to a large percentage of the public. This point stands for most of these locations, and is part of the reason they are enjoyed so widely due to their convenience.

Bottesford Beck

More often known as 'the Beck' to locals, this walking route is located at the end of Scunthorpe in the adjoined village of Bottesford, facing the village of Messingham. At the end of last year, it was announced that a visitor centre would be put into place at the nature reserve that will be named 'The Bottesford and Yaddlethorpe Education and Visitors Centre'.[3] Though the area is popular with ramblers, dog walkers and families, the new plans hope to further increase local tourism will encourage exploration of wildlife and the local area.

The Beck itself flows as a stream and connects to the River Trent. When the full walk is followed, the path leads to its partner reserve of Ashby Ville.

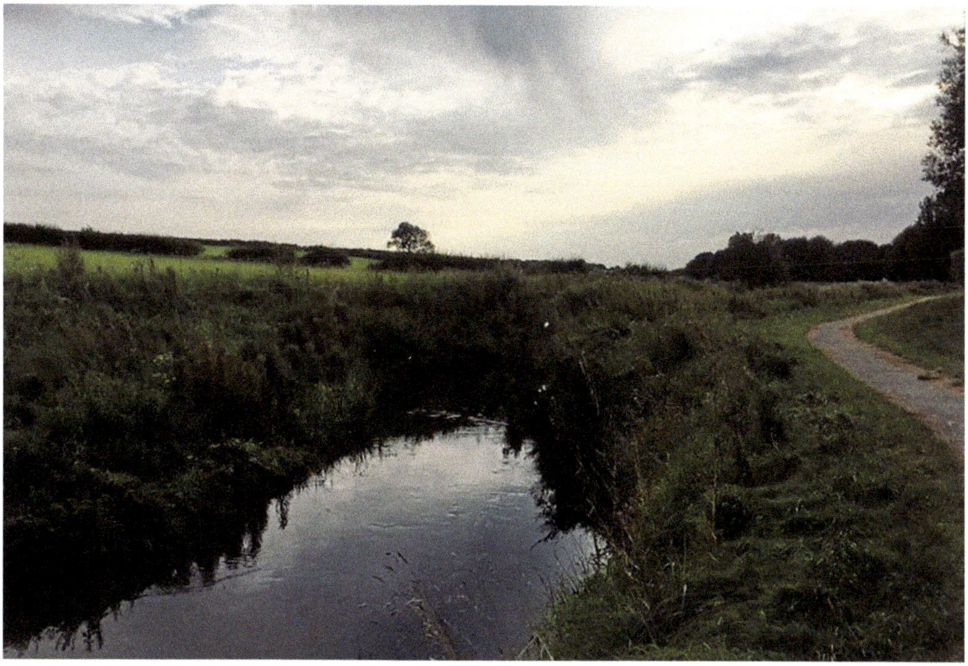

The area is an enjoyable secluded environment.

Silica Lodge Lake/Fishery

This lake is located at the north side of Scunthorpe, near to Bottesford, and is associated with the Silica Lodge Garden Centre located nearby. The lake is a popular area for fishing as is the fishing lake nearer to Burringham. Many visitors choose to walk around the lake due to its sandbanks and the 'island' that has been gradually formed.

Within the town of Scunthorpe many other areas dedicated to open space exist, often between housing estates that are designed for residents to enjoy. While it would be not appropriate to list all of them, it should be mentioned that these spaces provide the same enjoyment as those dedicated to the larger gardens. Spaces such as these supply a place to spend an afternoon, as well as being a popular site for dog walking and family activities. For some who live on one side of Scunthorpe, it is perhaps not as easy or accessible to plan and spend a day at Kingsway Gardens, for example. These other parks fulfil this role while adding to the idea of preservation and public services for all. Nearly all of these areas are managed by the North Lincolnshire Council, who commence routine gardening to maintain the standards not only of the local area but the public spaces we enjoy. Many of these parks and open greens are situated close to schools and places associated with leisure and popularity, providing a comfortable environment for everyone. Though Lincolnshire itself is (and is indeed known commonly) as a green county, Scunthorpe's gardens, parks and open spaces certainly adhere to the stereotype. The town is charming by many standards and though some may paint a poor image of it due to Scunthorpe's industrial aspects, once you begin to strip down the connotations of these opinions, you begin to see its true form: picturesque.

5. Sports Culture

The Scunthorpe's sports industry has been, and remains, an important and valued part of the town's culture. After the establishment of iron production it was deemed necessary to have an element of recreation that residents of the town could engage with and enjoy. It was not only those who worked at the steelworks that would need a break or hobby from their occupations. With the success of Scunthorpe's steel, many new types of industry had set up in the local area and all of these new workers needed an activity to look forward to since the level of hard manual labour is high within the area. When many think of the town's sport industry, it is not impossible to guess that their first thought would be of its football club. While football is indeed a large part of Scunthorpe's reputation and the most popular sport, we shall widen the focus here to include those that do not get as much attention.

Football

This is by far the most celebrated sport of the town and is especially enjoyed by many members at the local football ground of Glanford Park. Away and home games take place at the park on alternate weekends, attracting crowds of fans who hold the tradition of attending pubs while walking to the west of the town attending the game.

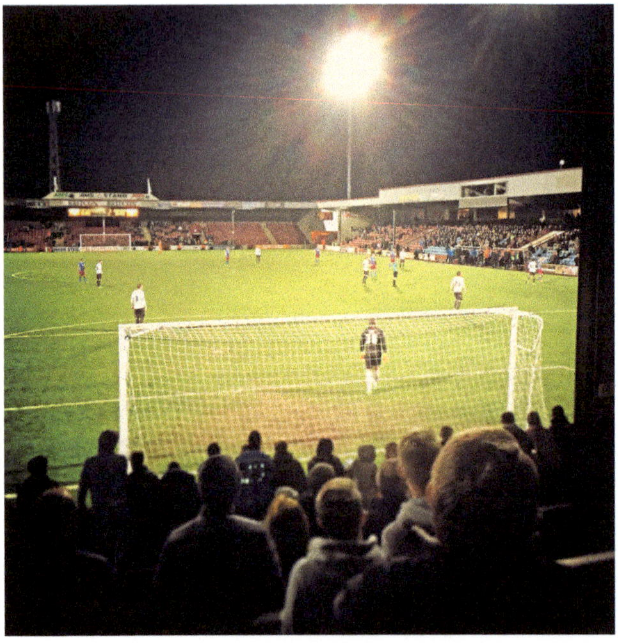

One of Scunthorpe's winning games last year. (Courtesy of Central Line)

Scunthorpe United Football Club (SUFC) is believed to have been moderately established around the 1880s while the town was begging to have its first surge in modern development; however, official figures suggest it was closer to the year 1900. Although the club today contrasts a great deal to when it was first established, the team has survived over 100 years from when it first began playing matches against the surrounding villages after two local villages joined together. Many small clubs representing villages and towns such as Winterton and Brigg played against each other regularly to establish who held the best team. During the early years of the club, Scunthorpe and its nearby opponents formed the North Lindsey League and began to engage in proper League games against each other. Scunthorpe joined with Lindsey United to form a stronger duo and increase their chances at making it professionally, and became known as the Scunthorpe and Lindsey League, though this was to be later removed from the club's name.

DID YOU KNOW?

Scunthorpe FC's colours became claret and blue in the years between 1904 and 1905. Some say that was an intentional attempt to mimic those of Aston Villa.

In 1950, Scunthorpe United joined the Football League after it had finally performed well enough against similar clubs, despite the fact that its rivals still remain clubs that are close within the Lincolnshire county. The club plays primarily within the League One division, although it has suffered numerous fluctuations in its position since it became a professional team. Its stand today has a capacity of a little over 9,000 fans, though it has recently received planning permission to build an entirely new stadium in the near future. After battling on its own for a number of years, the team acquired its fitting nickname of 'The Iron' in correlation to the town's iron and steel production. Many fans even still refer this nickname today, and the club's logo is in fact a fist holding a bar of iron.

Rugby

The pitch based on Heslam Park is a common sight in the Brumby district, the home of Scunthorpe's rugby teams. The club has not always been based at the park, instead begining as a small team playing on agricultural fields for small matches and training. These fields were formerly rented out to the players in exchange for a small sum of money, which meant that the fields could be simultaneously used by the owners to grow crops and raise livestock since the fertility of the land is vitally important. However, in 1952 the Scunthorpe club gained its own grounds – the rugby club had found its home.

DID YOU KNOW?

Heslam Park is named after its owner, J. R. Heslam. Mr Heslam was recalled to have donated the land to the team so that they would not have to continue to play on fields and constantly have to move around if they were unable to have a match.

Many of the club's players and interest came from the influx of workers after the war period had passed and a form of stability had been established. This increase in the population had also likely provided bigger crowds at the local football games, making the sports of Scunthorpe much more popular than before. Today this attention to the rugby team has remained popular. Heslam Park has a number of competitive teams, and the club has indeed come a long way from its founding in the late 1920s.

Heslam Park is also the base for Scunthorpe's cricket club. Surprisingly, the club was established when the area had its first modern boom at the end of the nineteenth century, having its roots in the town's formation and initial foundations. It is likely that the formation of Scunthorpe helped the development of the cricket club develop further, but even today the sport is relatively popular among all ages. In recent years the teams of the club have performed well, making their way up the cricket leagues gradually. The club has its own modified version of Scunthorpe's coat of arms; it shows a cricket player in action instead of the usual wheat at the bottom of the shield.

Cycle Song

Although the Cycle Song itself was not actually an event of sport, it was designed as both a celebration of the sports within the town and life of the town's own community. The orchestral performance took place in 2012 next to Brumby Hall behind Central Park on the open land used for sports. The sold-out event was dedicated to the Brigg-born cyclist Albert, frequently known as 'Lal' White, an Olympic Games silver medallist who was famously known for playing in Antwerp. The event featured the integration of many creative groups and was intended to focus on the entire community of the town and its surrounding areas. Not only this, but perhaps more importantly, the showcase demonstrated that the feature of the steelworks and the lives of those within in the area have always been intertwined as the custom-made set featured a depiction of the steelworks and the town's skyline.

Lal was a former steelworker in Scunthorpe and his achievements showed the importance of sports to the town, but also that he came from a bustling and supportive community. As I remember myself, many children used the park as a way to see the show over the fencing. The attention attracted over those two days of its performance was outstanding. The musical, dramatic and sporting sides of the town all came together over those days to remember life and achievement – perhaps a perfect summary of Scunthorpe.

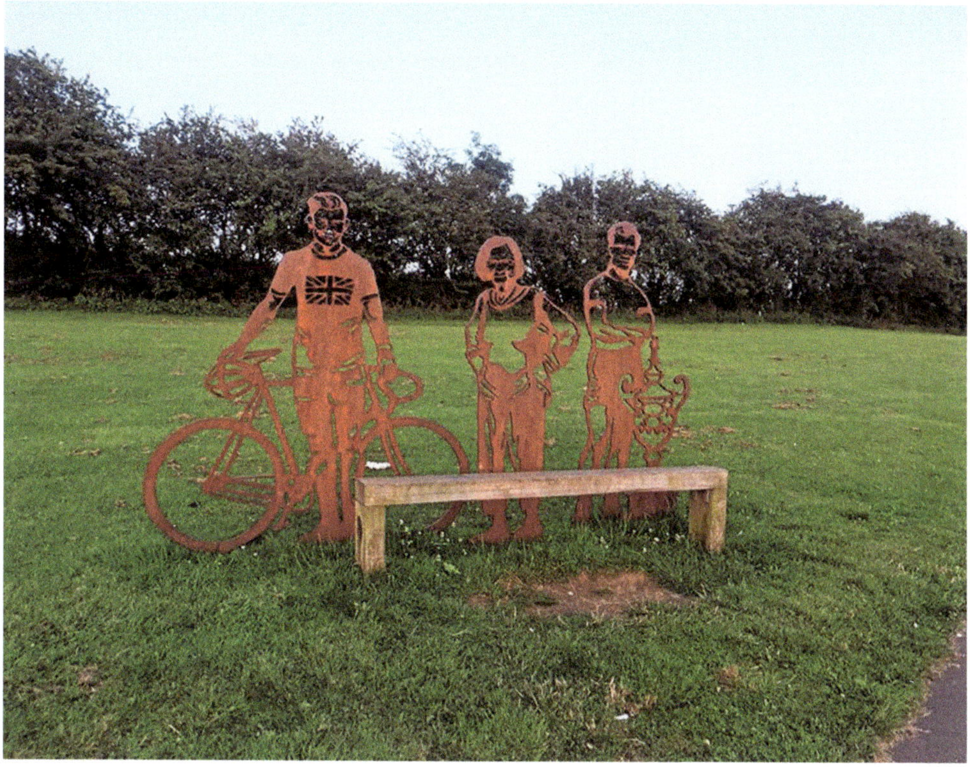

The running track, Velodrome and stadium. (Courtesy of Paul Harrop)

Quibell Park Stadium

Based next to the viaduct on Scotter Road, Quibell Park is one of the only open spaces for many athletes to train and compete against each other. The park is a venue where various sports take place, including athletics, cycling, field events and occasionally football. The track is surrounded by a velodrome in which track leagues are held weekly for those involved within the cycling community of North Lincolnshire. Schools especially use the site for sports days and practice events, and, due to the large open grassy spaces, the park is usually an ideal ground for events such as Armed Forces Day due to its size and capacity.

Unfortunately, the stadium has been under construction for a while after a fire damaged the property earlier this year. A large amount of money is being invested in order to restore the building, which has remained quite unchanged since its first opening and will help to resurface the running track and other parts also destroyed.

In addition to Quibell Park Stadium, the Pods leisure centre opened over five years ago and is now sometimes used as a replacement ground for those affected by the closure of Quibell Park. The leisure centre was an investment designed to encourage the uptake of sports within the town and, based next to the Council House and Central Park, it is in a prime location within Scunthorpe.

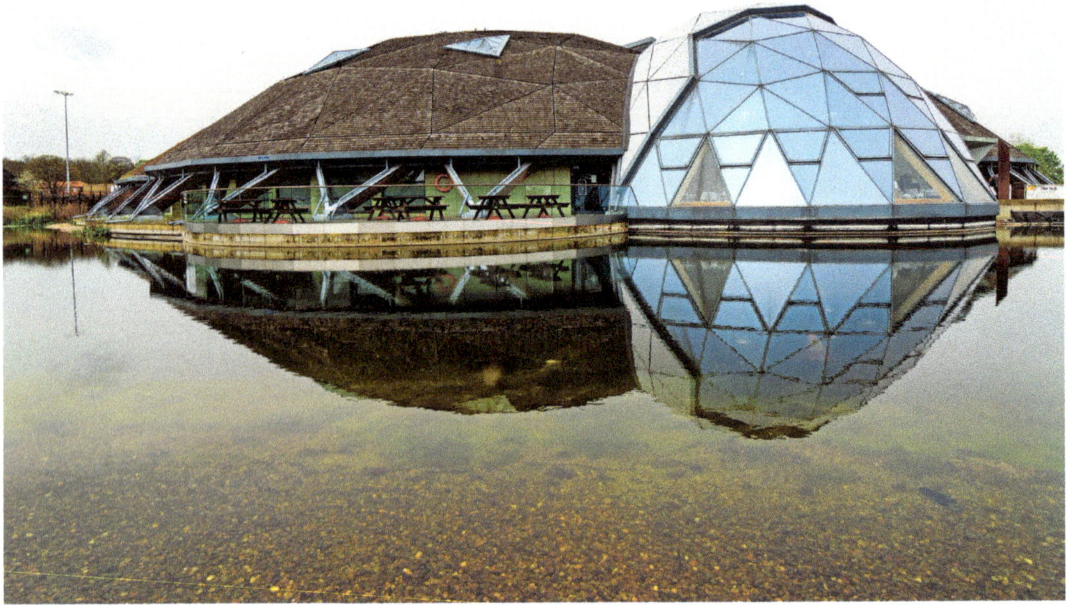

The Pods, located next to Pitwood House. (Courtesy of Simon Reinhardt)

These sports are, of course, not the only ones that exist within the town. As much as it would be interesting to analyse every single type of athleticism within the local area, it is not practical to do so. There are many other types of sport, depending on your individual classification of what such entails. The bowls community here is quite popular with the older generations of the town, and events are quite often held at indoor or outdoor clubs, or even the occasional pub that has its own pitch. Golf is also an example of another relatively popular sport; Ashby Decoy, Holme, Kingsway and Forest Pines are all examples of the many golfing greens within the area. All of these states, as well as others, focus on the draining capabilities in order to offer the opportunity to play in almost all weathers. Many were founded at the start of the twentieth century, which corresponds to the population increase in Scunthorpe, similar to other sports. Perchance a point about the town's sport culture should be that the capabilities to house so many types of sport in comparison to the size of the town is actually quite tremendous. These sports could not take place without the land that they are based, and the drive to provide an open space with flexible land demonstrates the dedication and support of the local industry. Many of these sports join places together because of their geographical locations and the crowds that they attract, while others serve as integration mechanisms for separated villages by bringing interests together.

6. Pubs and the Search for a Footrail

Every place that we visit, if they happen to be small villages or entire cities, will usually have at least one pub. This does not mean that they become unimportant in their abundance, but rather they tend to blend in with their local environment and merge as a setting. Before the rise of sports and theatre within Scunthorpe, pubs often served as the former alternative for entertainment. Many pubs within the town still serve this purpose, and many residents will have their local favourite. This section is designed to reveal some of the history behind some specific pubs, as well as maintaining the tradition of their entertainment culture. While it is impossible to include every single pub within the town (this section would likely become tedious for many readers), I hope that I have succeeded in my attempt to capture some from the former traditional townships of Scunthorpe by reaching out into the areas they exist today. It is, of course, without a doubt that many pubs that would be exciting to visit today and explore their histories have unfortunately been demolished or replaced by something new. That being said, the first section of this chapter will be concerned with a few of those that fit this description.

The Queens Pub

It is unfortunate that some places of local historical interest have been closed down or no longer exist; the Queens pub is one of those places. The pub still stands today on Rowland Road, near to the town centre, but is now rented out.

Some locals recalled that the pub served the best breakfast in the town. It was a very popular place to be, bustling with both local customers and visitors from all over the

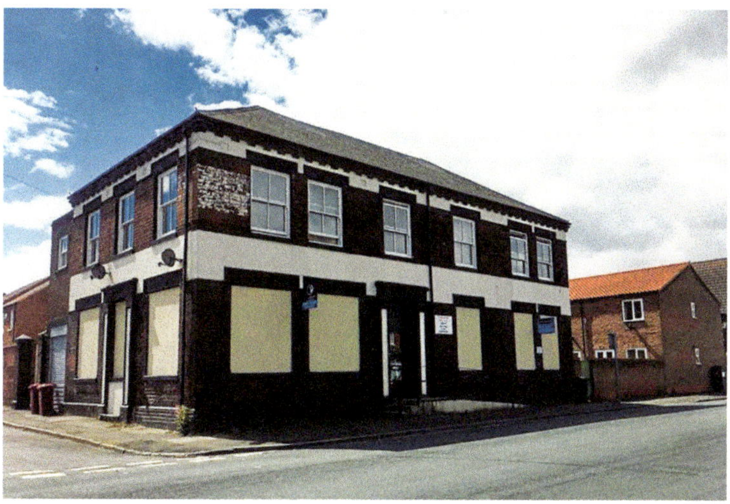

The pub is located in what was a once highly popular area.

district. The area was, as previously mentioned, perhaps intended to be busy for the building of a high street, and the popularity of it seems to support this. Its closure is rumoured to be due to a lack of business, and when you visit the areas around Rowland Road, it sadly seems to be a true conclusion.

The Coronation Club

While it lives next to its neighbour the Queens on Rowland Road, it is also said that the pub was a popular site for people of older generations who enjoyed a beverage in the evening and at weekends.

It is rumoured that during the war the Coronation was used as a makeshift mortuary in an attempt to contribute towards the war effort. While the pub was still open, there were many pictures of the First World War covering the walls inside. The pub was formerly a working men's club, although it is likely to have suffered the same fate as its partner next door. The venue is currently looking for a new owner to restore both its history and potential to develop an area of bustling business.

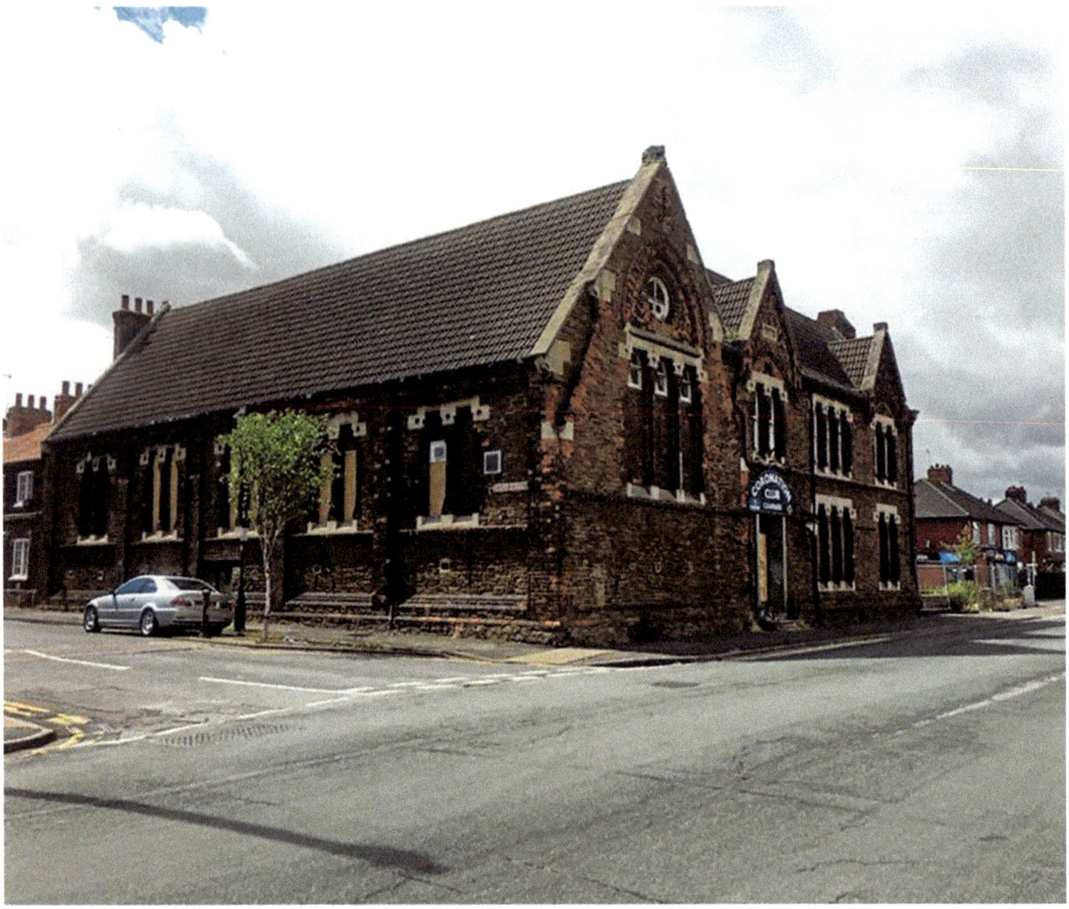

The Coronation pub was a hotspot for some time.

The Oswald/The Tavern

Built in the Victorian era, the pub is situated today in the town centre and is quite often a popular choice for those who live nearby. Though it is now known as The Tavern, the pub is definitely one of the oldest in town and is rumoured to be possibly the oldest in the centre.

If this is in fact accurate, it would likely explain the popularity of the pub, not only because of its location in the heart of the town but being the first of its nature it was always likely to have attracted attention.

The Furnace Arms

The Furnace Arms will be a place many people who have lived in Scunthorpe for a while will remember, but many are unaware of its existence due to its demolition almost twenty years ago. The former pub was also located in the town centre and many remember it to have been a popular place for steelworkers to have a drink before or after their shift (frequently, I believe, in both situations). Before its demolition, its name was changed to one completely different to steel production. The nightclub Club 2000 was built in its place near to Church Square at the far side of the town centre.

It seems that the pubs around Scunthorpe have formed a theme with regard to their naming, often being associated with steel and royalty. Pubs or venues that fit this latter description include the Crown, Queensway, Mary Rose, the Royal and the Queen Bess. Many others include the town's legacy of steel production, and most familiar with Scunthorpe are likely to be able to think of at least one associated with it in some respect. The fact is that many pubs have found their roots in the existence of local steel production, but this does not mean that the lack of an important production site would mean a lack of pubs, rather their existence provides a feeling of purpose and pride. In the early days of the industry many pubs would specifically open at an extremely early time (perhaps 5 or 6 a.m.) for workers leaving a night shift or beginning a day shift to have a pint. It is with ease, therefore, that we are able to understand why so many pubs are named in association with the great works; it is also interesting to see how much the works influenced the running of such pubs.

Highfield House

Highfield House may also be taken as a hidden beauty or gem in accordance with its concealed location within the town. Though the pub is relatively large, it is similarly located in the town centre, but near to the police and railway stations unlike others.

The house is based on a large ground and features a sizeable bowling green, where matches or practice often take place. The pub was formerly a working men's local, strikingly comparable to many others in the town, and is today part of the Sam Smith's pub chain. The pub allegedly served as a base for a certain Trade Union Club headquarters for a number of years, though observing its history it is perhaps likely that this may have been a Labour or steelworkers' union. It is rumoured that Highfield House was built for the chief ironmaker at the Steelworks, George Tosh. Perhaps this was intended for him to live in at some stage, or maybe to own himself one day. Regardless, it was simply a quiet place after a long shift. The building was apparently built by apprentices as a project,

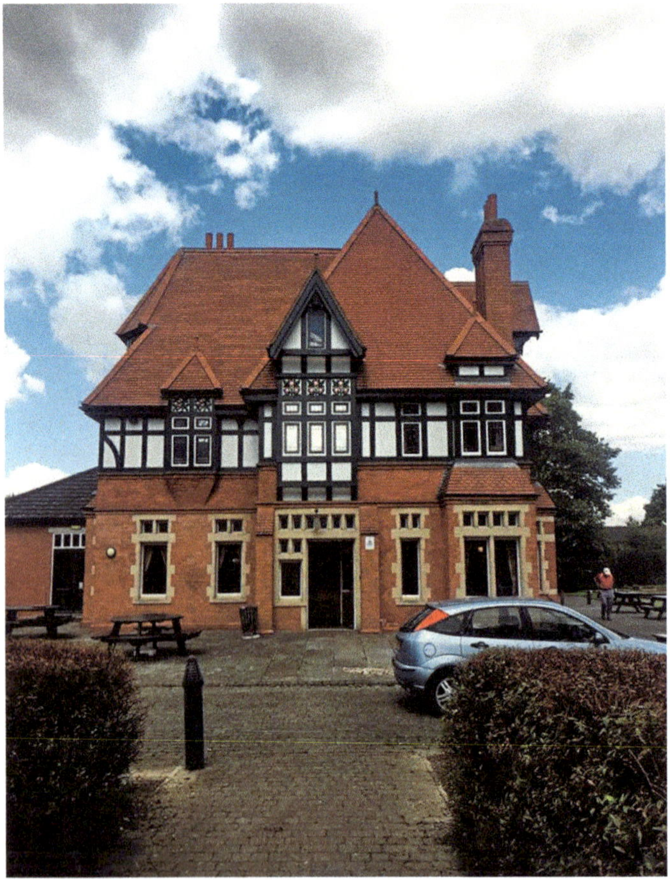

This gorgeous building is, surprisingly well hidden.

though it is unknown whether the handy work was performed just by these apprentice builders as a way to secure a cheap labour force and therefore a lower cost production. Highfield House is built in a Victorian Queen Anne style, part of its distinctiveness comes from the unique sunflowers weaved into its architecture on the exterior panels.

Malt Shovel

This pub is relatively peculiar, yet homely both in its inward and outward appearance. It is quite frequently referred to as the country style or village pub in Scunthorpe, which is most likely due to its roof and décor.

When speaking to some locals of the pub and some of its staff, I learnt that the pub was actually once a cinema. The first cinema was called The Globe, with its roof shaped into that of a dome, which you can still see today if you take a walk upstairs. After The Globe, the cinema became known as the Roxy. The front of today's pub was formerly a ticket entrance, while the back (where the fireplace now is) was formerly the Roxy's screen. After its cinema days the venue became a bingo hall, where many would attend in an evening during the week. It was then adapted into the style we see it today to become the local village pub in Ashby.

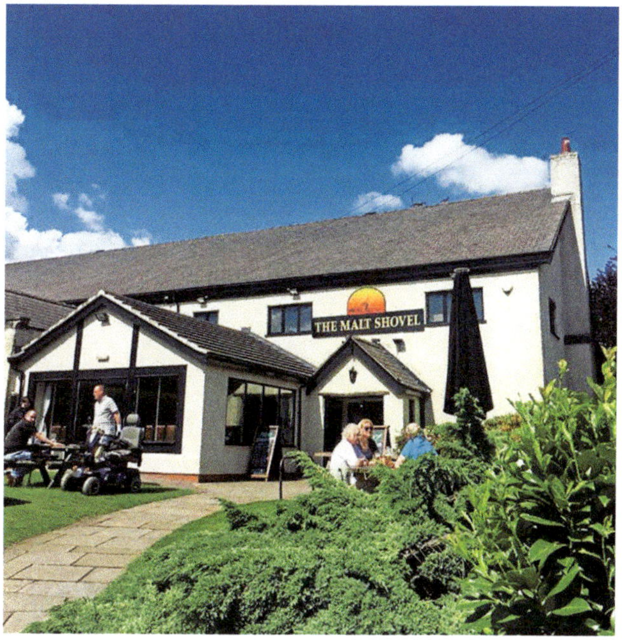

The Malt Shovel.

The Berkeley

The Berkeley Hotel is a common sight from the west entrance to the town and is located at the bottom of the roundabout Berkeley Circle.

Built in 1940, it was named after Sir Berkeley Sheffield and its interior is decorated with old pictures and memorabilia celebrating his life and association with Scunthorpe. The hotel is a Grade II-listed building and has been preserved well to avoid deterioration. Sir Berkeley was not only an MP during his life, but during his younger years he also served in the Lincolnshire Regiment as part of a commitment to his county.

DID YOU KNOW?

It is rumoured that, similar to other pubs in Scunthorpe, the Berkeley was used as a makeshift hospital during the Second World War. This would make sense as the pub is located on the outskirts of the town and is of a relatively large size, making it easier to access in comparison to pubs in the town centre.

Scunthorpe and the areas around North Lincolnshire have a little amount of relation when warfare is concerned in comparison to larger places such as Leeds or Sheffield, but perhaps the more significant aspect is that people from our community have been involved in those events. The Regiment is known today as Royal Lincolnshire and has been recruiting since the late eighteenth century. Its quarters are quite rightly based at Lincoln and it has had a significant contribution to the military history of Britain.

The pub was planned and styled according to the works of Mrs E. Kennedy, who has a distinctive style. Each room, including guest rooms, have a differing colour scheme. The hotel is still functional and features a daily food service with specials. Its ballroom is found by walking through the lounge area and is often used as a large venue. While the pub is of the Samuel Smith's chain, it is quite noteworthy that the prices of drinks not only in the Berkley but within the area are affordable. That being said, it is quite a suprise that when people (especially from the south) come to visit, they are taken aback from by the prices of ales. The Berkeley features Taddy largers and pure organic brews, as well as Bitter and Sovereign Ales as their popular beverages.

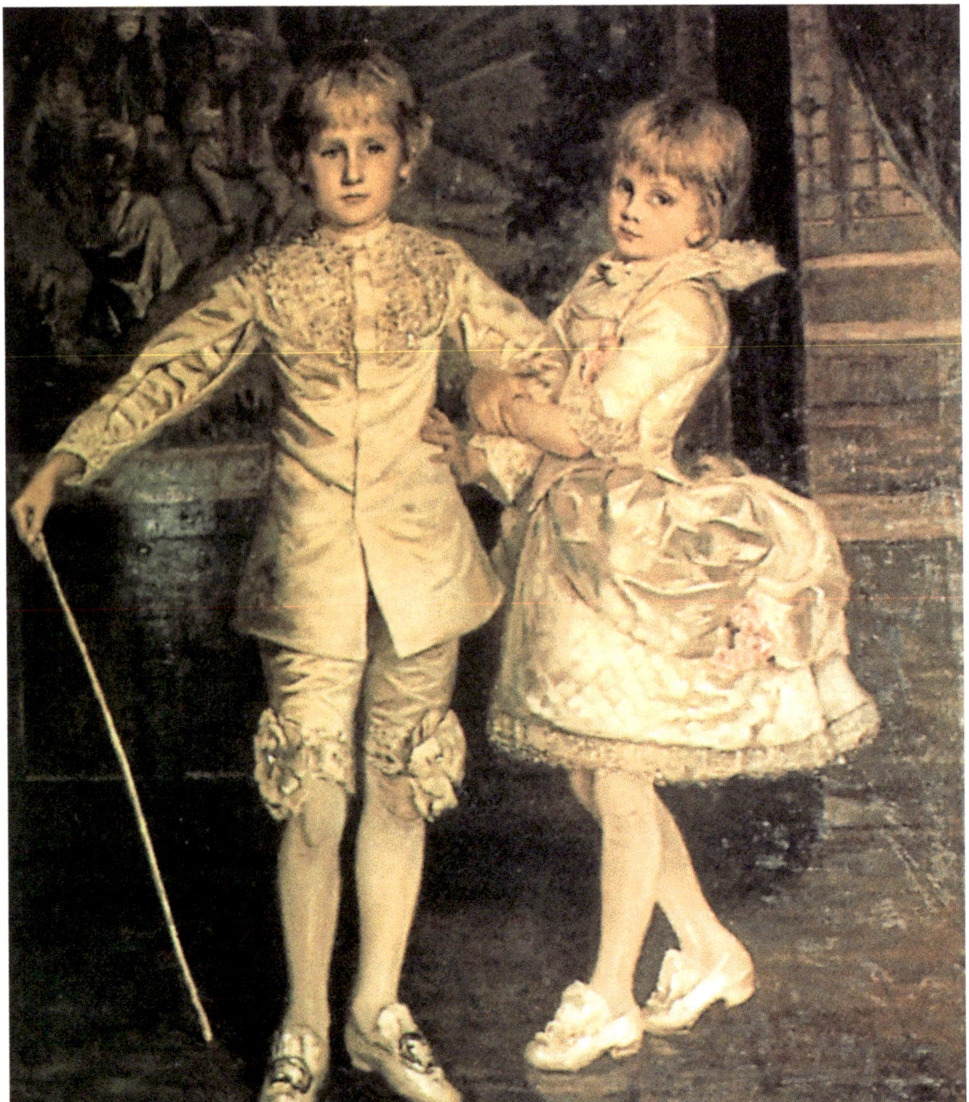

Other pictures similar to these are found inside the pub.

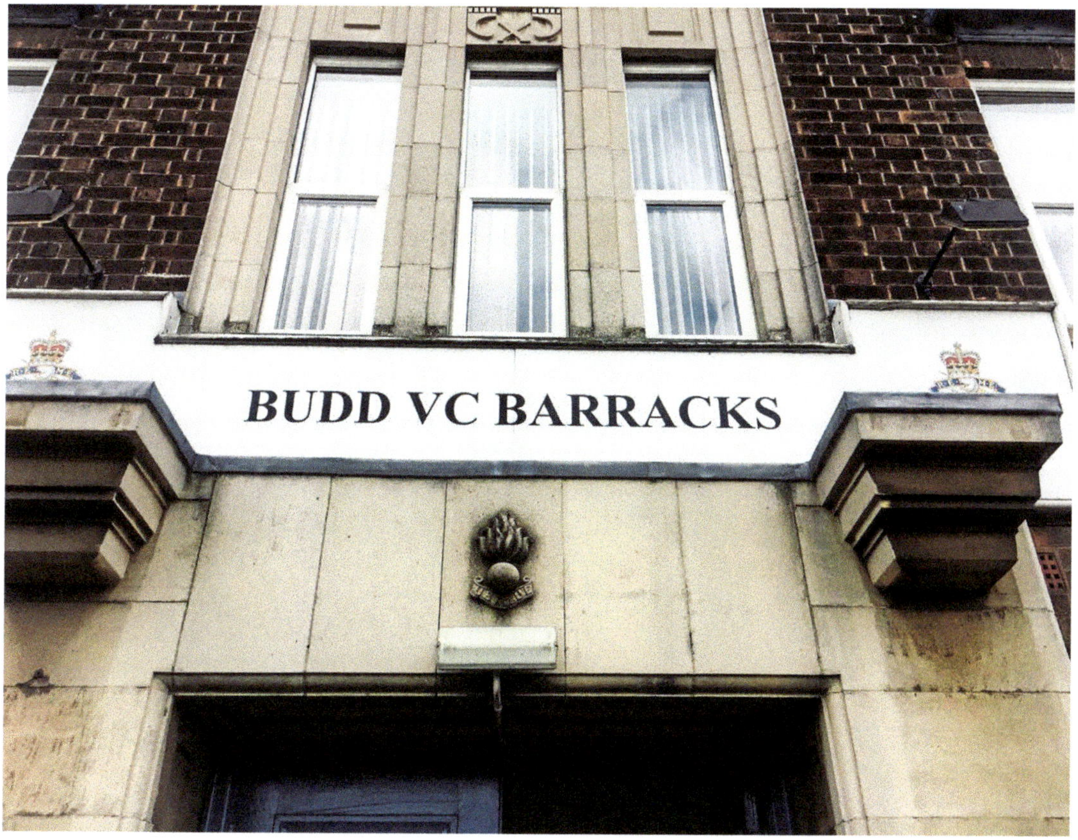

The barracks of Scunthorpe, Royal Lincolnshire Regiment.

Sir Berkley Sheffield was a Conservative MP and his father, Sir Robert Sheffield, owned the Normanby Hall estate. It is generally known that the Sheffield family are of some kind of local fame, which is perhaps unsurprising when good deeds such as Sir Berkeley building a school in Crosby are rumoured throughout history.

7. Religious Routes of the District

While we may not often notice the number of churches within Scunthorpe and its villages, the role many of these have played in the town's history is perhaps unacknowledged. During periods of lower prosperity and throughout the earlier period, few schools existed around the North Lincolnshire area. Most churches therefore stepped in to cope with the lack of education provided, thus playing a significant role in teaching children and others in need of education. Local sights of attraction are also part of Scunthorpe's heritage that tie to its religious routes and serve to provide local tourism and historical interest.

Church building began to increase at the end of the nineteenth century, in the same period monasteries were also branded significant. It was thought that the Yarburgh ecclesiastical divisions were of particular importance within the North Lincolnshire region, and played a vital role in religious influence. There is a surprising amount of churches within Scunthorpe; we may infer from this that the area had particularly deep roots in religious practice, but it is more likely that many were built in the villages of Scunthorpe before they formed to become the town we have today.

St Lawrence Church

This church, located on Church Street near Scunthorpe town centre, is situated within the Frodingham district. When looking at the earliest rectors of the parish, it can be estimated that the church existed in the mid-eleventh century, though it may have been built before this since it is typical for renovations to disguise the initial framework. It is common for partially incomplete or illegible records to belong to historical sites; therefore, it can sometimes present itself as an issue when attempting to pinpoint appropriate dates.

The tower is thought to have been constructed in the early thirteenth century, though it unfortunately suffered damage when the steeple fell in the early 1600s and was rebuilt. The church also features bells that have existed for nearly 400 years.

DID YOU KNOW?

The architecture of St Lawrence's Church archway dates back to the thirteenth century, but also features some Georgian displays due to its refurbishment in later centuries.

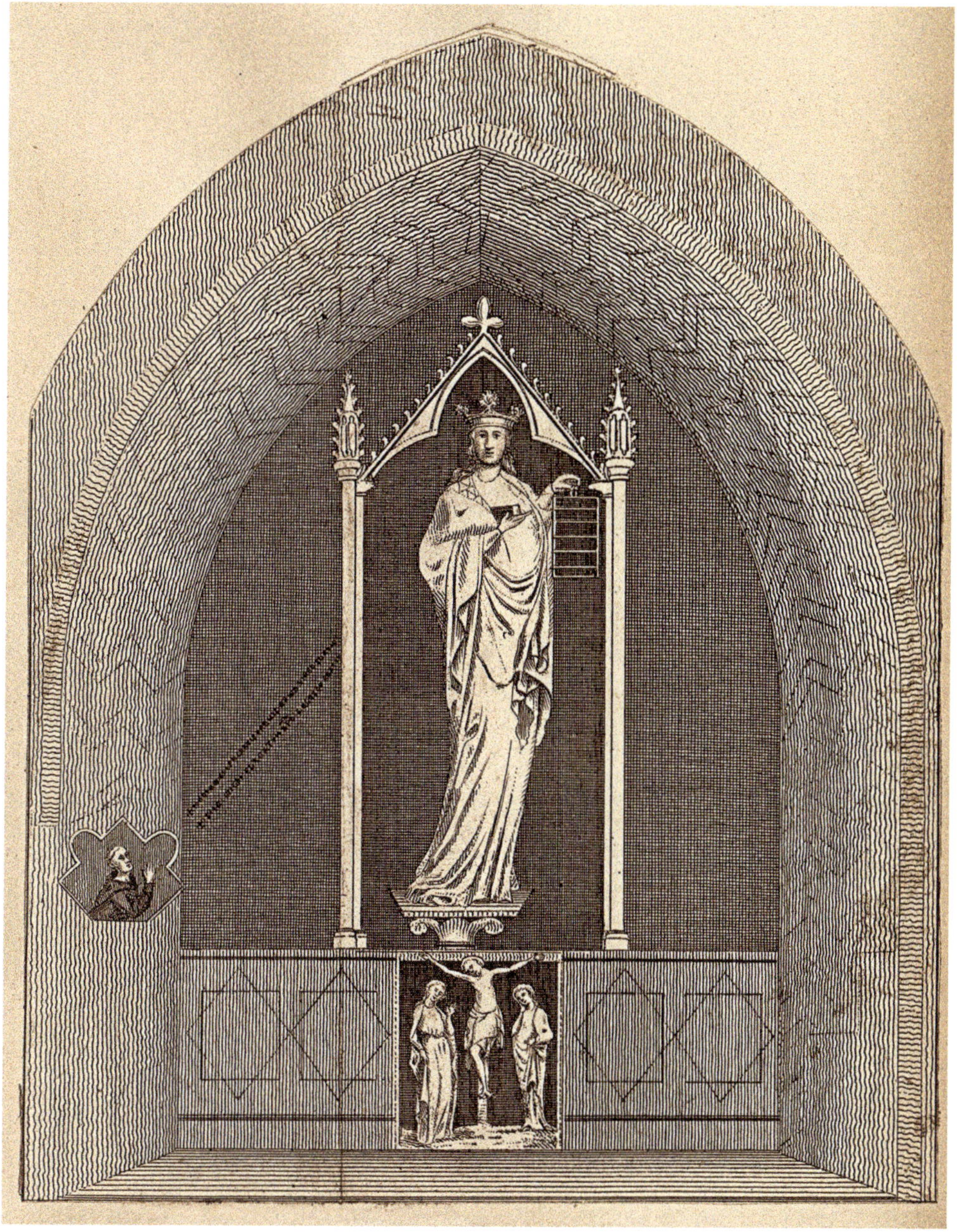

St Lawrence of Rome.

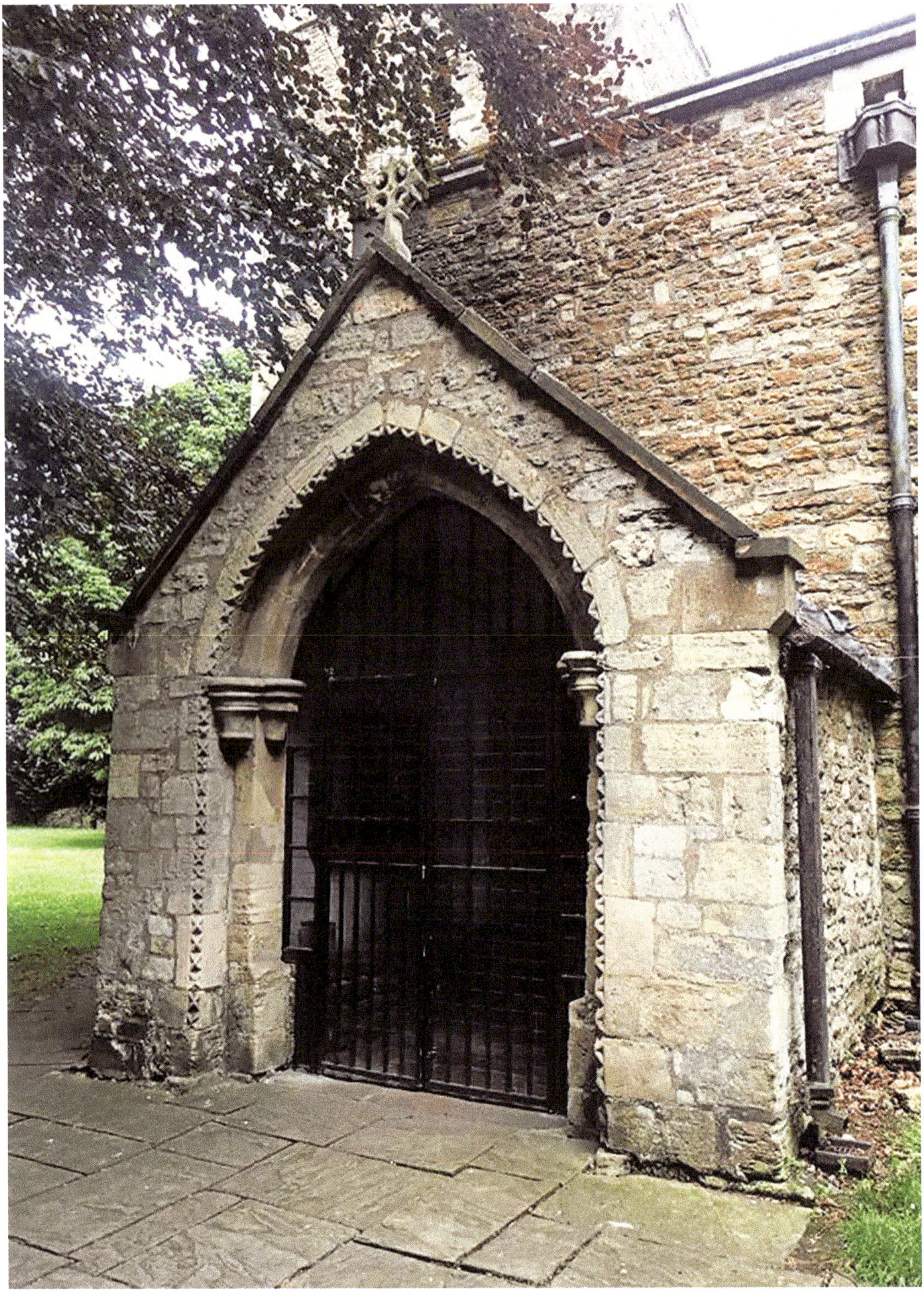

The classic archway, which often puzzles analysts.

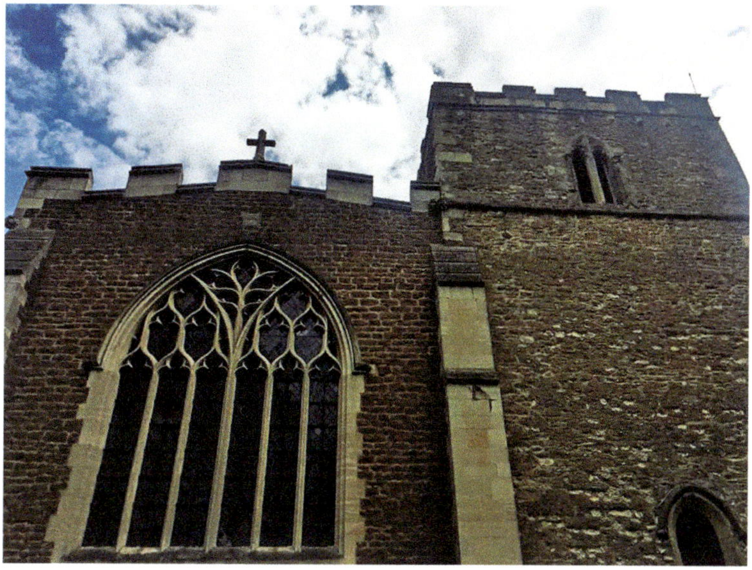

The whole church in view next to the museum.

St Hugh's Church

St Hugh's Church is a frequent sight for those who live around the Brumby district of Scunthorpe, known today as 'Brumby Corner'. The church is located on Ashby Road in a busy area between the directions of the town centre and Ashby High Street and features grassland and a small school inside its walls.

The church was built in 1939 during the local industrial and population boom. An interesting feature of the church is its tall tower and, more importantly, the swan that sits on its highest point. According to history, the swan is a significant symbol of the church's saint: Saint Hugh of Lincoln. He adopted the swan as a friendly pet, and the swan guarded him as he slept as his protector.

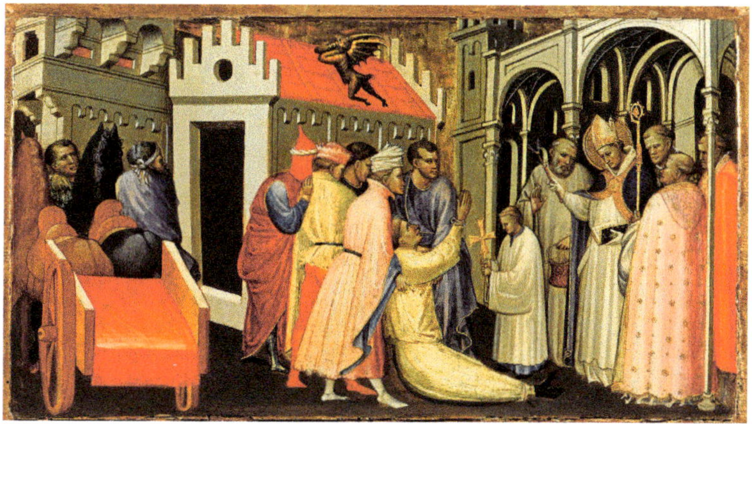

A depiction of St Hugh the Bishop performing an exorcism.

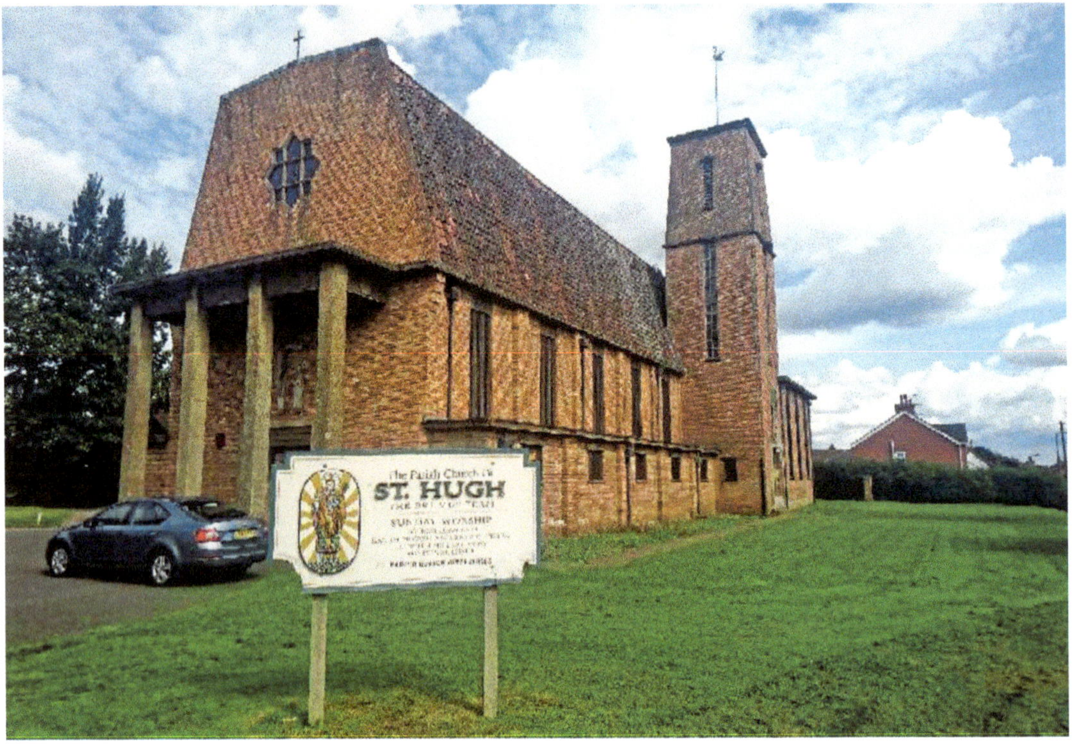

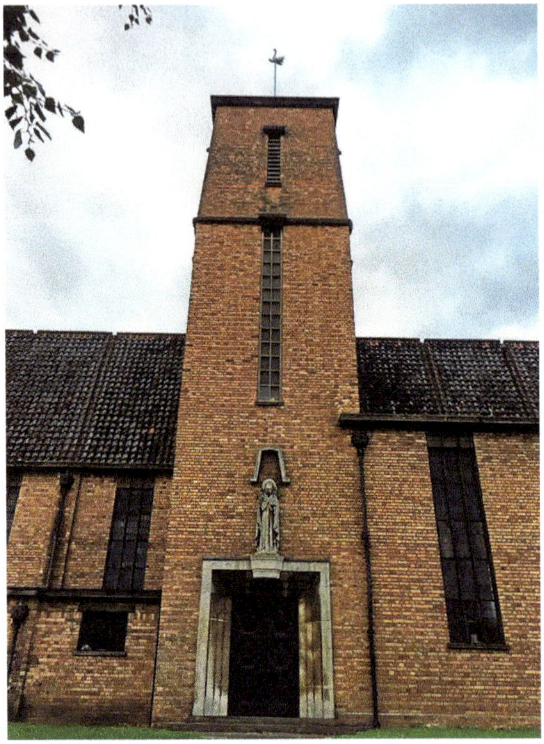

Above: The Parish Church of St Hugh.

Left: The duo are stationed at the highest point.

St John the Evangelist Church/Nos 20–21 Visual Arts Centre

The visual arts centre in the heart of Scunthorpe is often hidden away, though the majority of residents are aware of its existence. Nos 20–21 are actually the renovated Church of St John the Evangelist, built in 1891. Though the centre is not a typical church, it is seemingly a unique and interesting one to include.

> **DID YOU KNOW?**
> The Church of St John is actually built from the ironstone sourced in Frodingham, and became a very successful church when it was used.

For a while the church was not in operation, and so it remained empty without purpose. Luckily, by the year 2000 work began on the old church in order to renovate it into the arts centre it is today. The church was reinforced and new areas were built, connecting it together to become a united piece for visitors to walk through and enjoy.

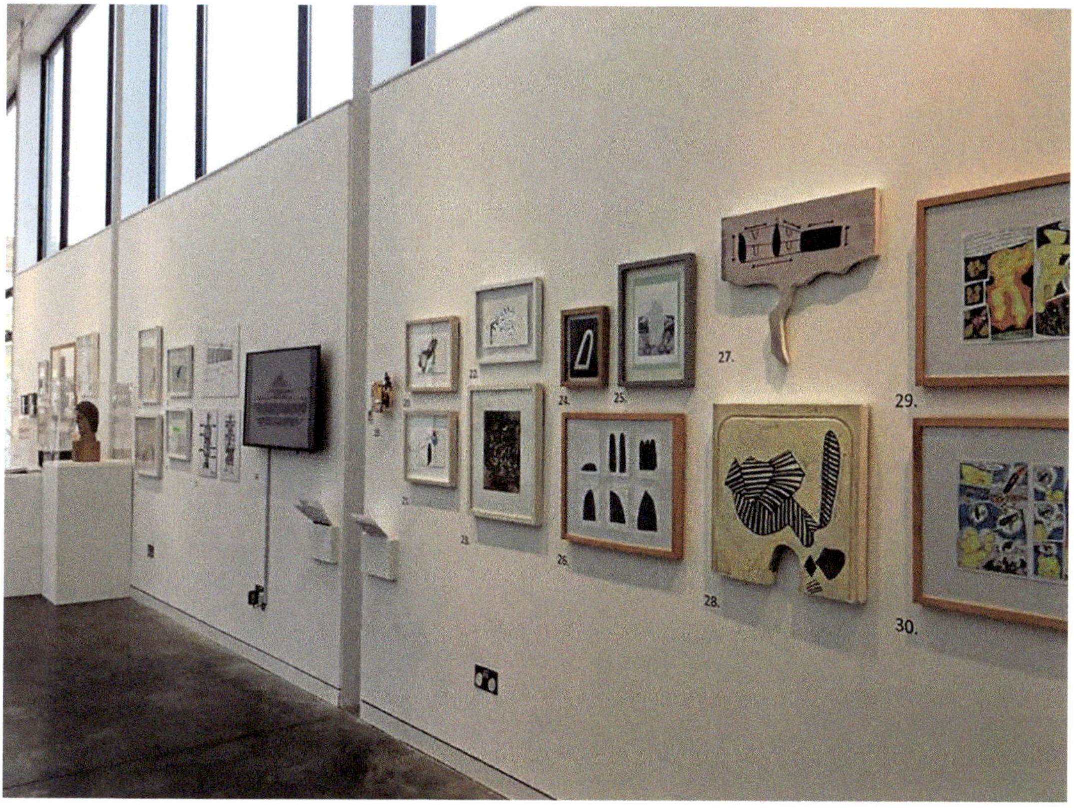

Some current exhibitions inside of the gallery.

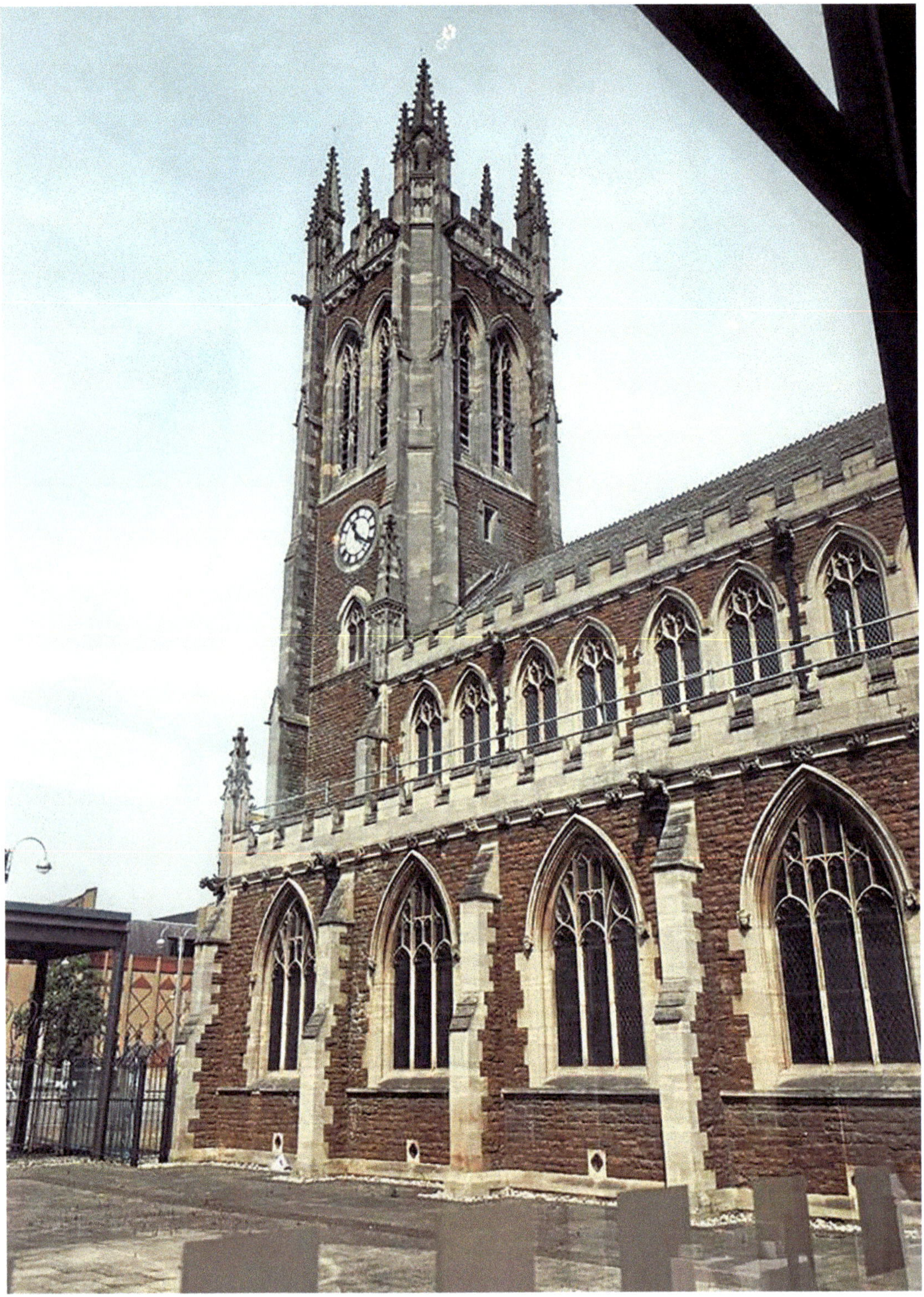

The arts centre is based inside of the church.

The name of the building has always remained an aspect I had always thought interesting but never fully considered until this point; it signifies the fact that the project of its refurbishment was started in the twentieth century and finished and opened to the public in the twenty-first.[4]

St Peter's Church

Though St Peter's Church is located in the parish of Barton-upon-Humber, situated at the very top of North Lincolnshire, close to the Humber Bridge, it remains an important element that links to the close history of Scunthorpe. The Anglo-Saxon church features a tower and architectural work that are stereotypical characteristics of churches built within the Lindsey area. Graves within the grounds of the church also date back to the Anglo-Saxon period but others date back to various other ages, making the site a local interest and attraction.

English Heritage now take care of St Peter's Church and protect its history, preserving the church and maintaining its events and opening.

In close proximity to St Peter's Church is St Mary's, the parish church of Barton, which dates back to the twelfth century. Not only is the distance between the two churches interesting, but so is the precise and fine detailing on and within them. Both churches have been preserved incredibly well and feature intricate doorways and windows designed to appear striking when the light hits them from within. St Mary's is more likely to catch the attention of onlookers simply because its appearance is slightly more presentable, despite that St Peter's is, in theory, greater is historical depth.

It is unknown why the two churches were built so close together. Some have speculated that religious tension began within Barton, while it may be the case that St Peter's became too small in comparison to the number of people wishing to worship.

It is interesting that in total there are three churches near to, or within Scunthorpe, that are all dedicated to Saint Peter. Saint Peter was known to be a follower of Jesus (one of the Apostles), hence why in many of his sculptures or depictions he is often placed in close proximity to him. As a result of his worship in early Christianity, as well as traditional Roman practice, Peter is considered an important saint. Due to all of these churches dating back to a similar period (around the eleventh century), it is perhaps a sign of traditional Christian practise and attitudes within the Saxon period. The church in Alkborough also possesses a tower dating back to the same period.

The first of these is found at Scotter, just past the village of Messingham towards the south of Scunthorpe. The church is part of the South Manlake group and also includes other churches in the nearby area such as Scotton and East Butterwick. Part of the interesting history behind the church is the different historical periods associated with its architecture and some of its objects. Similar to other churches in the area, the doorway is estimated to date back to the eleventh century – quite often due to their robust structure.

The Grade I-listed building has Norman and Saxon characteristics and its tower bares close resemblance to that of St Peter's Church in Barton. The font inside dates back to around the fourteenth century. Its white interior is also an unusual characteristic of the parish – visitors are often surprised when they visit on a sunny day.

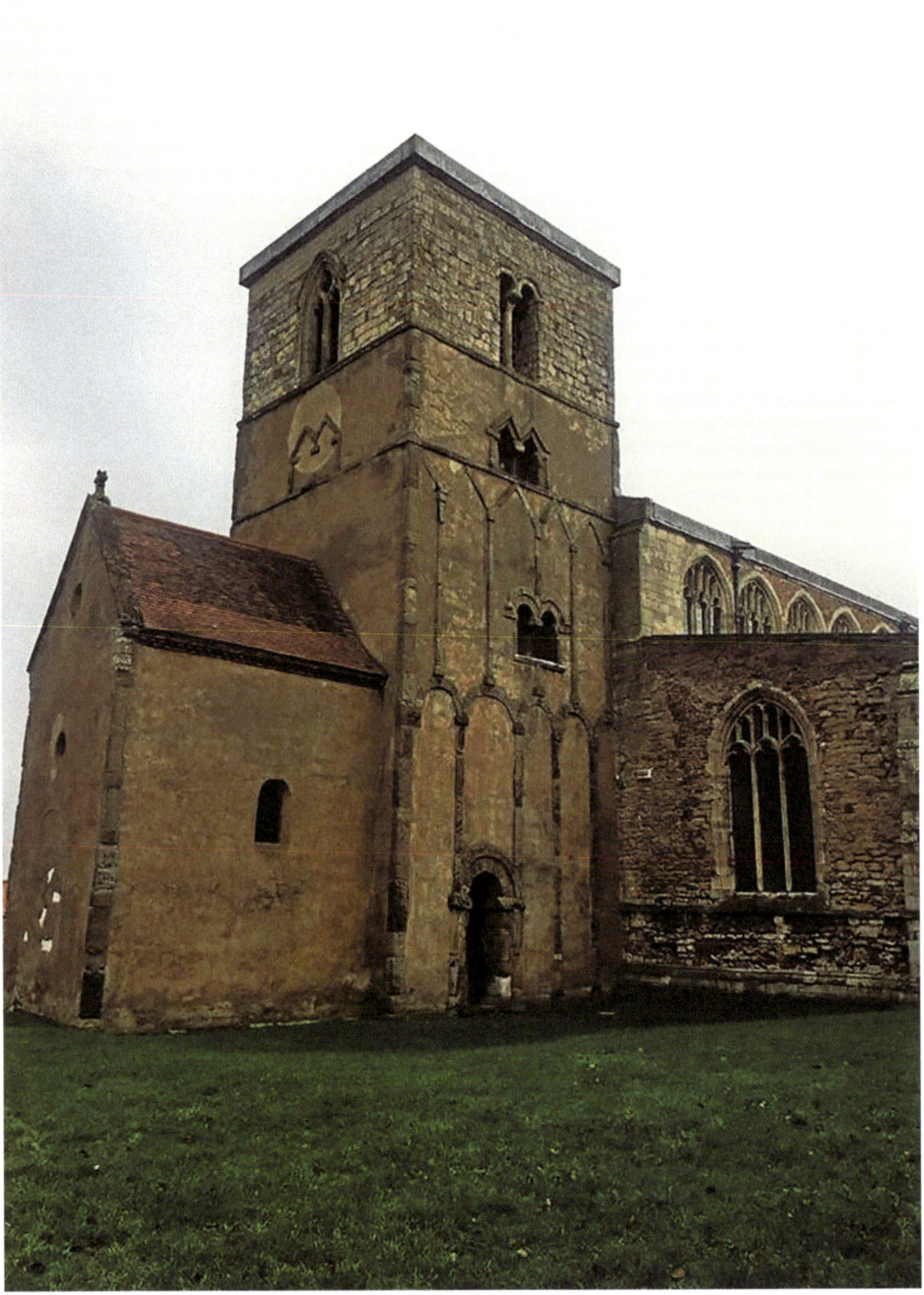

The profound English Heritage site in the Humber region.

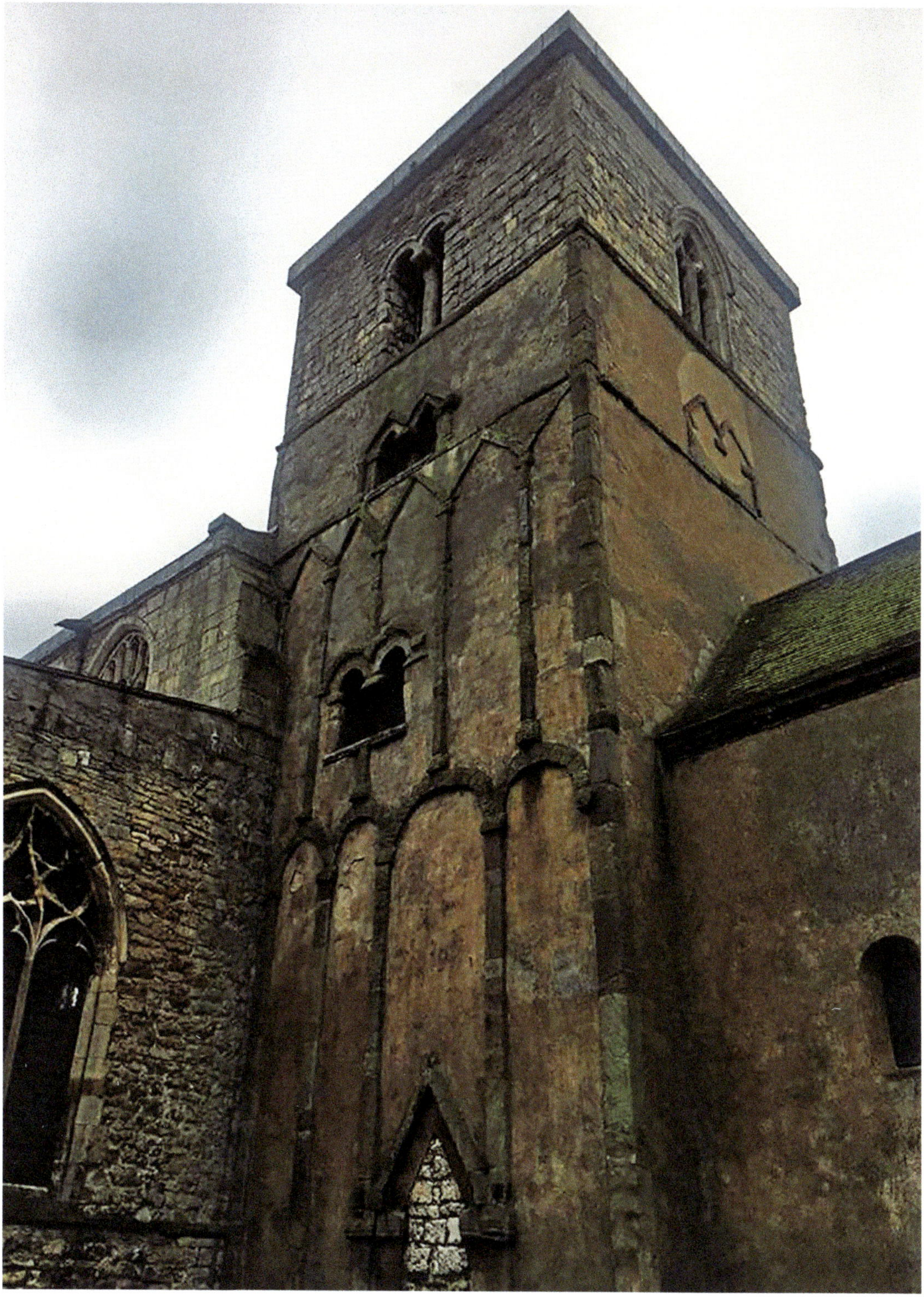

The tower of St Peter's Church is typical of its structure.

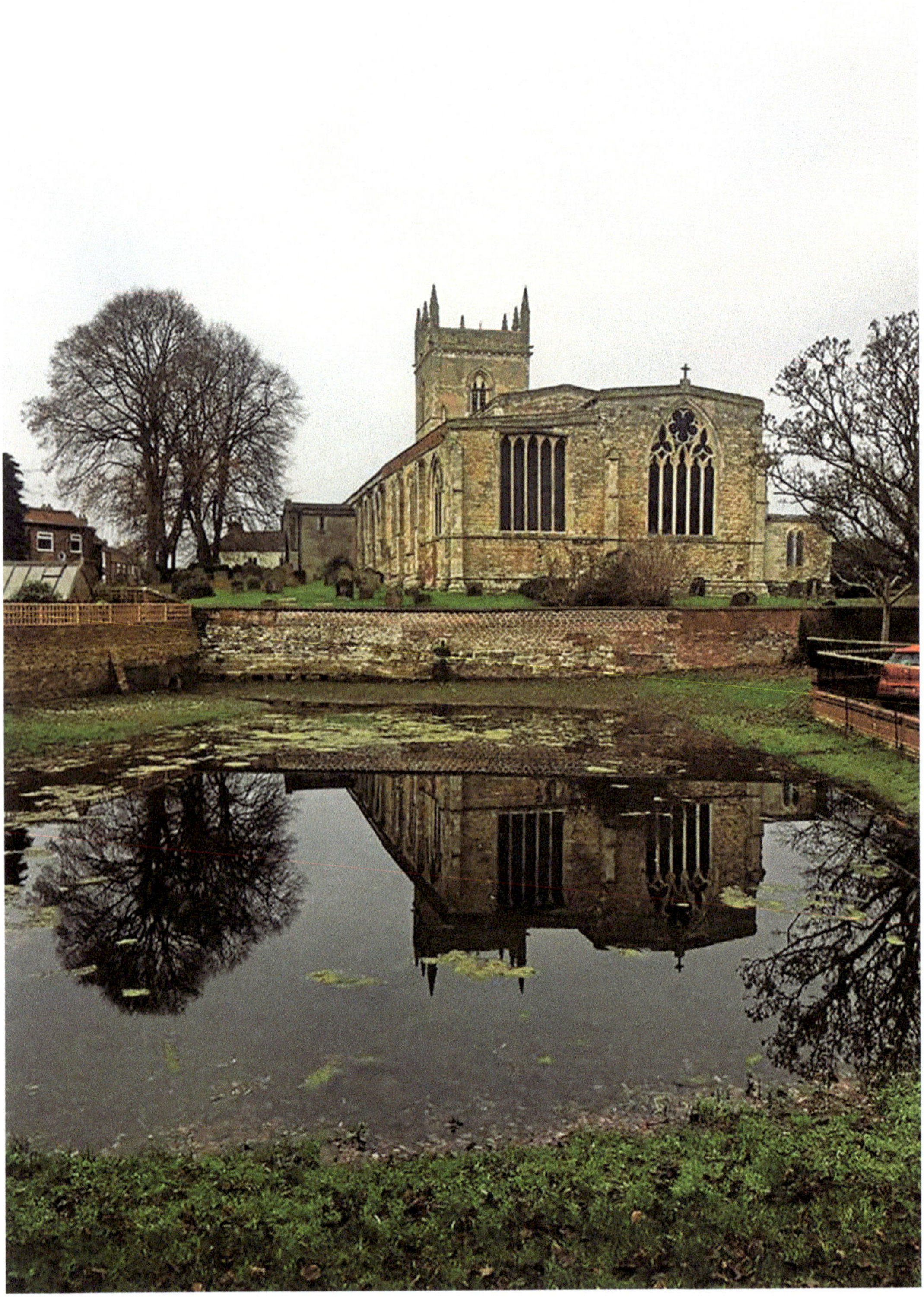

This church was in close competition with its neighbour.

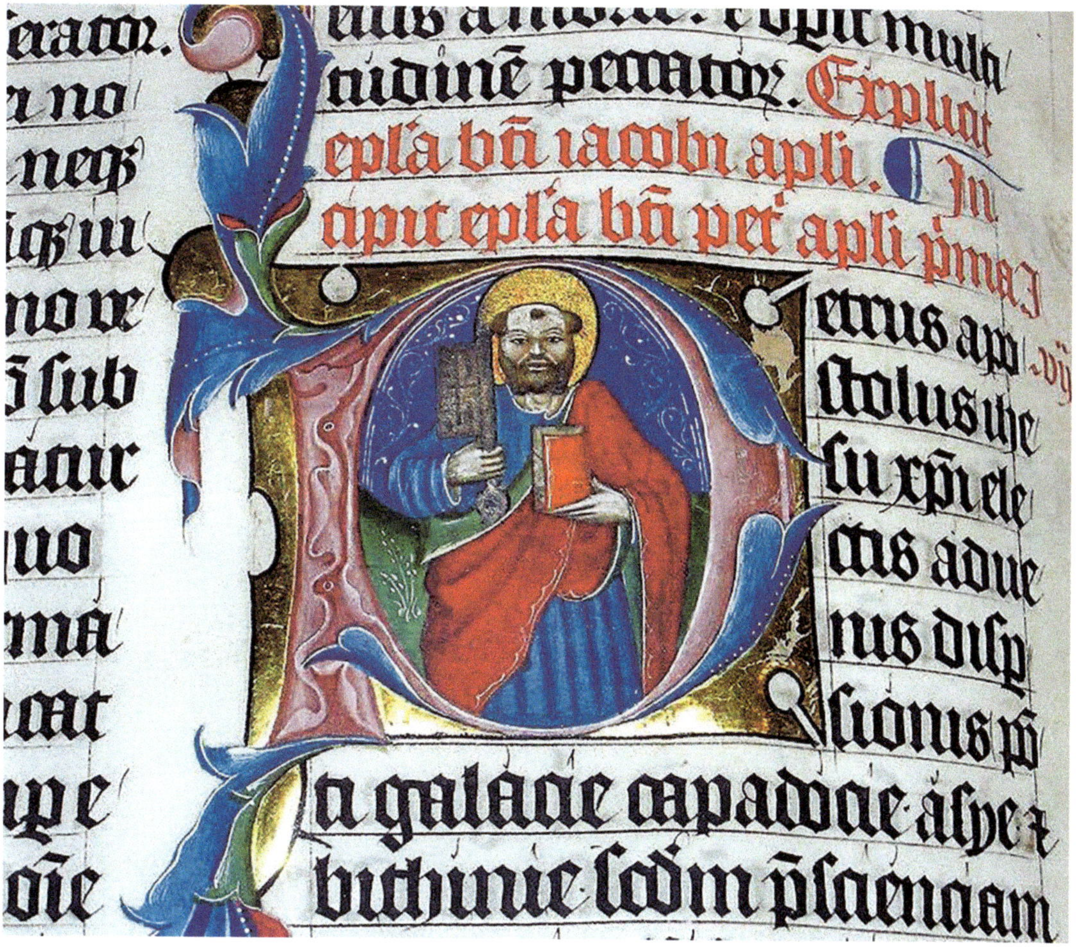

An illuminated depiction of Saint Peter.

The second Church of St Peter is found in the small town of Bottesford. The church's full name is St Peter ad Vincula, meaning 'St Peter in Chains'. The church is situated near to the Bottesford Beck and some public footpaths around the site lead to its gates as part of the area's nature walk.

The churchyard is set in a tranquil environment and features gardens that can be enjoyed by visitors to the church, even if they are secluded. This Grade I-listed building dates back to the medieval period, but the historical context of the town may suggest its history may be more similar to those of the two other churches of St Peter.

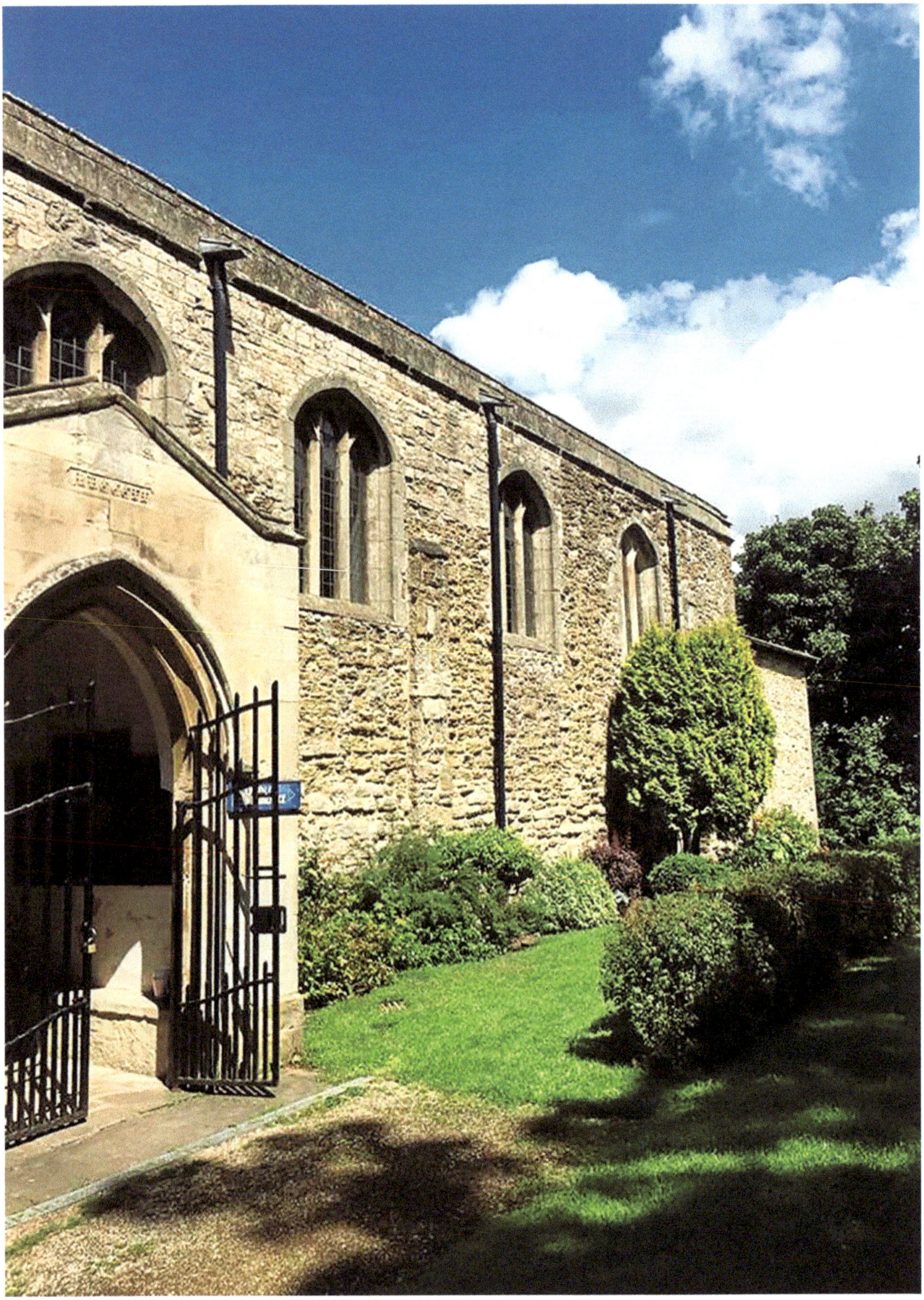

A similar, yet modern version of Barton's St Peter's found at Scotter.

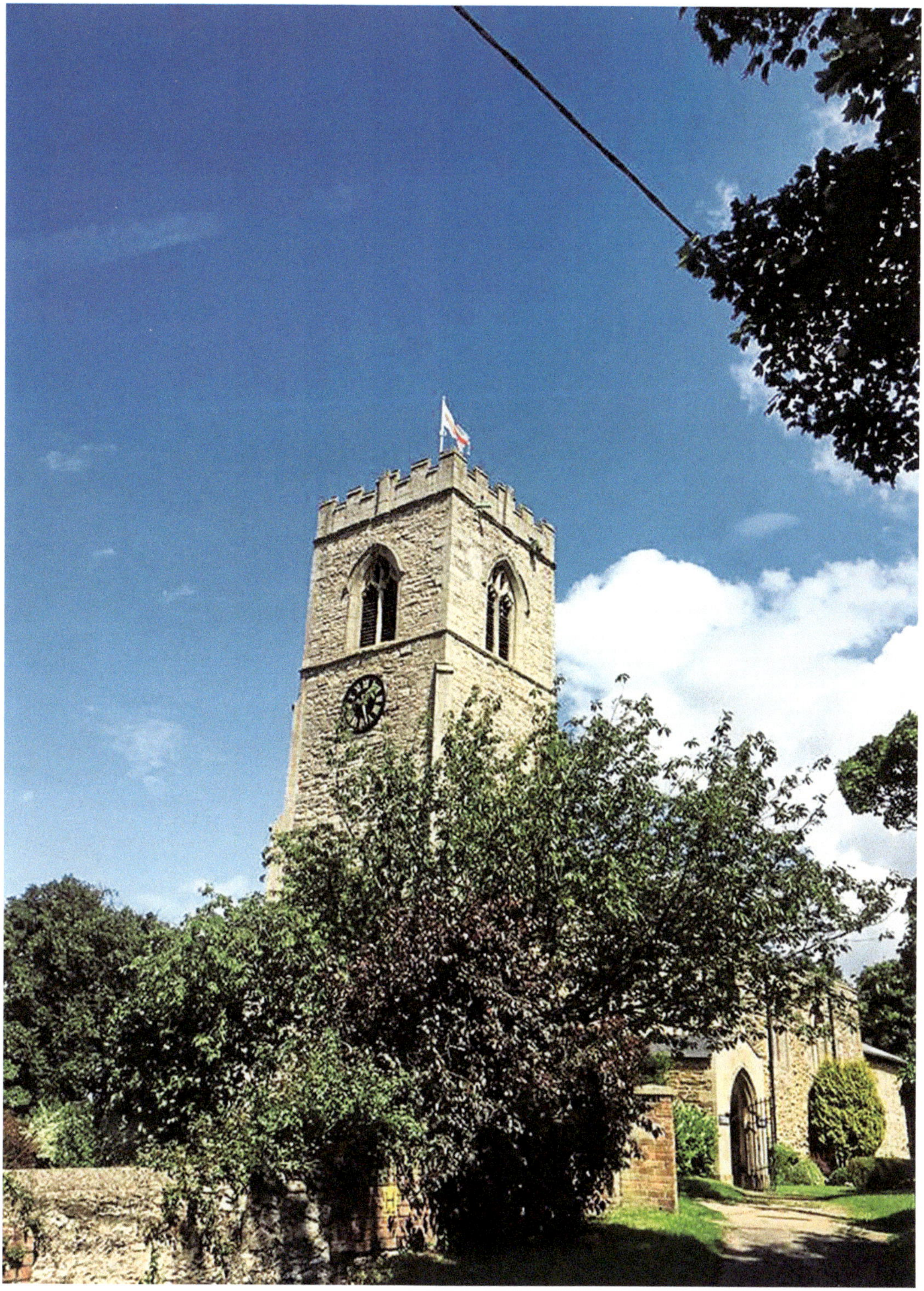

As we have seen previously, the towers are architecturally repetitive.

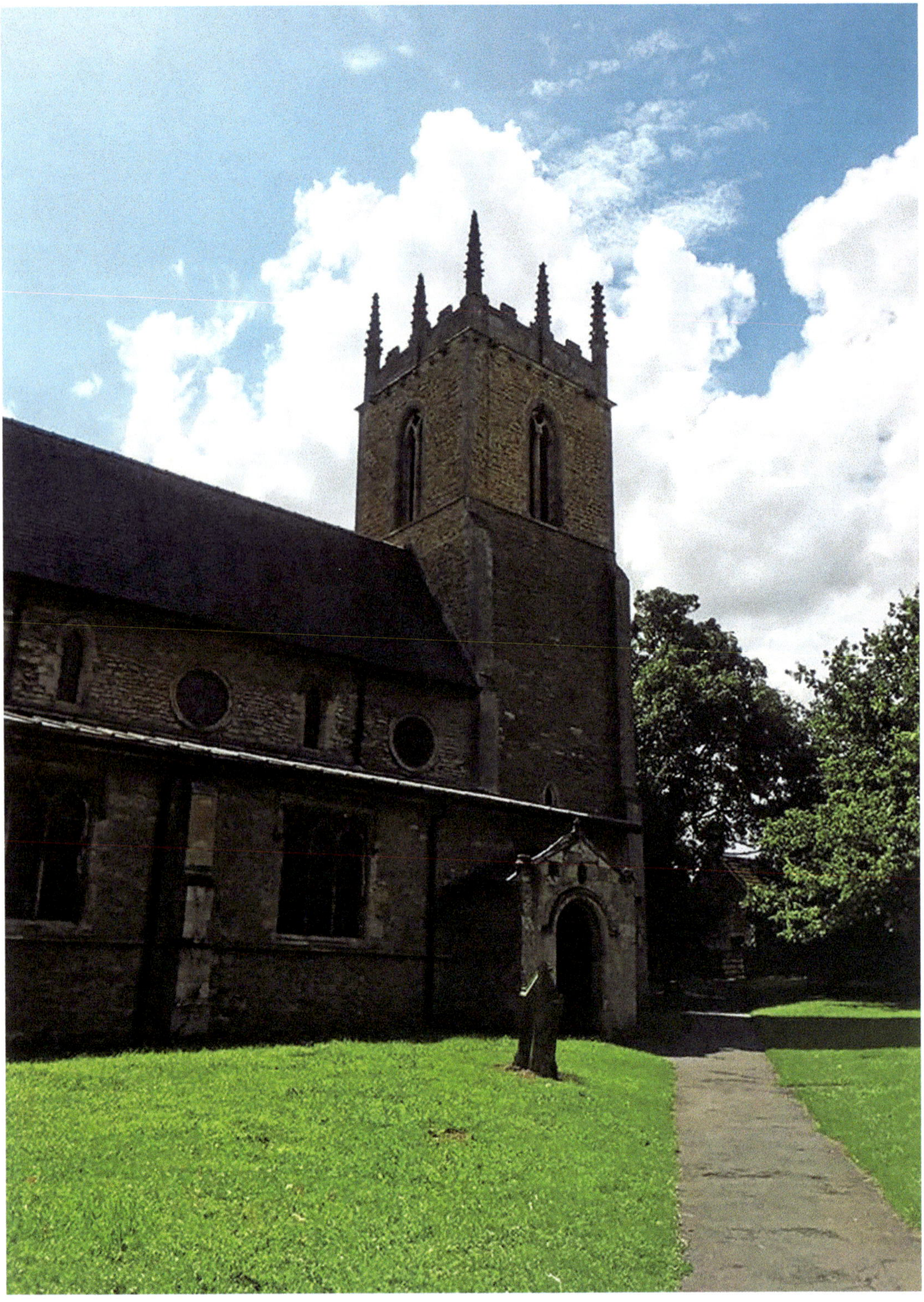

This church is out of the public eye, unlike the others.

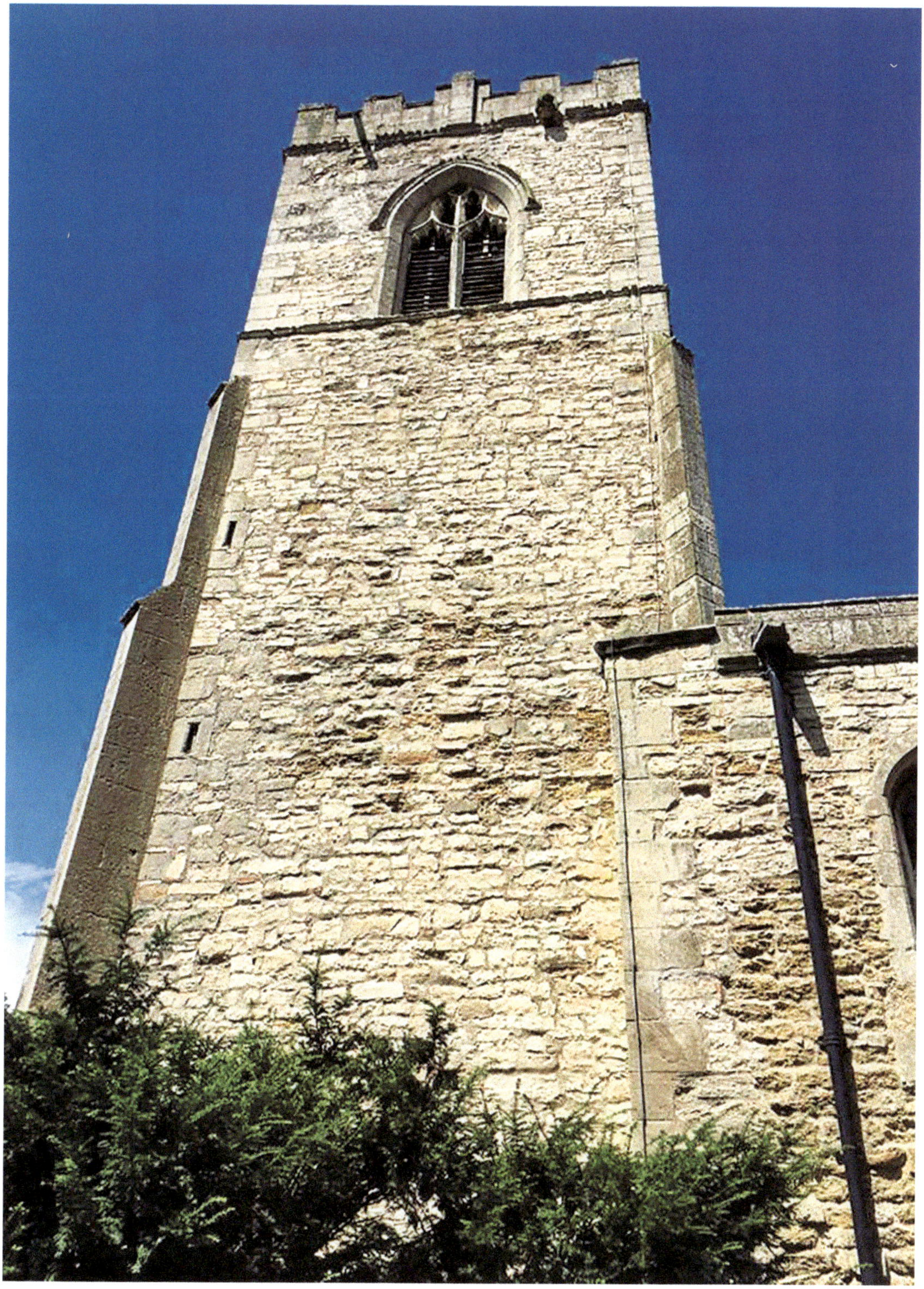

The building has been incredibly well preserved.

St Mary's Church, Wrawby

Wrawby is located just outside the town of Brigg near to a locally famous windmill, and provided a central place for religious worship in its local area. While all villages and Brooks in the Scunthorpe area have a church or chapel, Wrawby's church is significant in that it was the only one around Brigg until a local one was built quite recently.

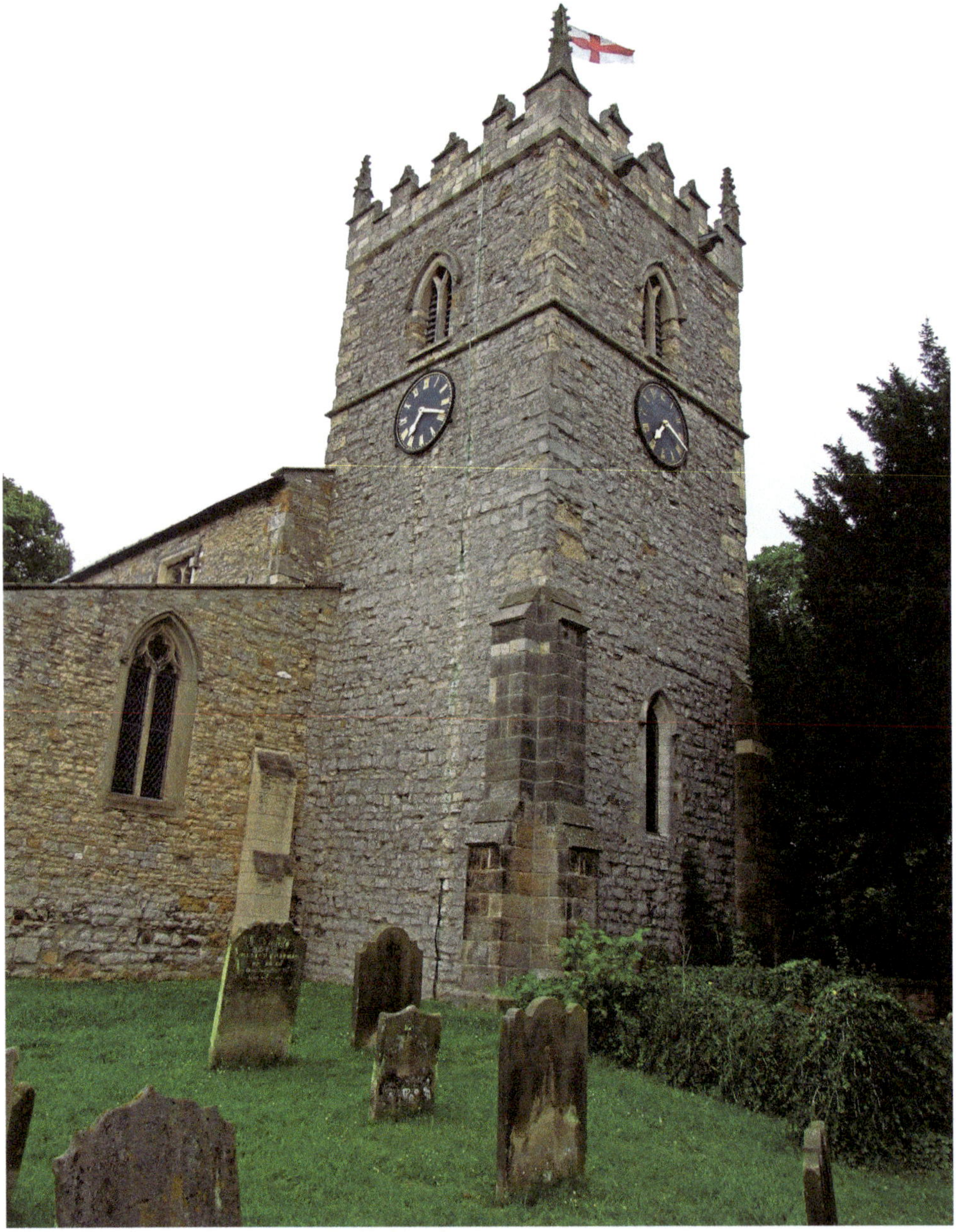

The Church of St Mary at Wrawby, featuring an intricate clock.

St Mary's Church is thought to have been of Anglo-Saxon origin, though its actual build has become murky due to many refurbishments and implementations. When the stonework itself is studied it is apparent that they date to differing centuries – most prominent around its archway and base stones. Important tombs are located within the grounds of the church and many have taken the liberty to study them. The church also holds or, more precisely, has held an alleged parish register, but it is thought that a fire a few centuries before destroyed (or at least damaged) it.

DID YOU KNOW?
Many of the churches featured in this chapter were built in a perpendicular style. This may be due to rebuilding work in later centuries to restore them. Others think that the style may have shown a common relationship in church planning, making the buildings more stable and sturdy against the weather.

Thornton Abbey and Gatehouse

The spectacular Thornton Abbey is thought to represent the spread of religious influence in the North Lincolnshire region, it is also supposedly the largest remaining gatehouse in England. The abbey is located near the small village of Thornton Curtis and is a popular choice for a day out in the North Lincolnshire and East Riding regions. It was completed in 1382. At present, the abbey and gatehouse is under the care of English Heritage, who restore and maintain their upkeep.

The gatehouse is fortified and features complex architecture as an Augustinian abbey. We are able to explore the insides of the gatehouse today. It is noticeable that there are stone figures on the outside of the abbey, which serve the purpose as an eternal dedication and form of protection to the fortified treasure. Jesus stands at the top of the gatehouse, while those of John the Baptist, the Virgin Mary and Saint Augustine lie underneath. As with many places of historical interest, it is probable that there were once many other figures but have unfortunately deteriorated through time.

DID YOU KNOW?
The abbey was able to avoid the Dissolution of the Monasteries by Henry VIII by becoming a secular college, turning into a place with little connection to religion. The abbey did, however, eventually close in the mid-sixteenth century.

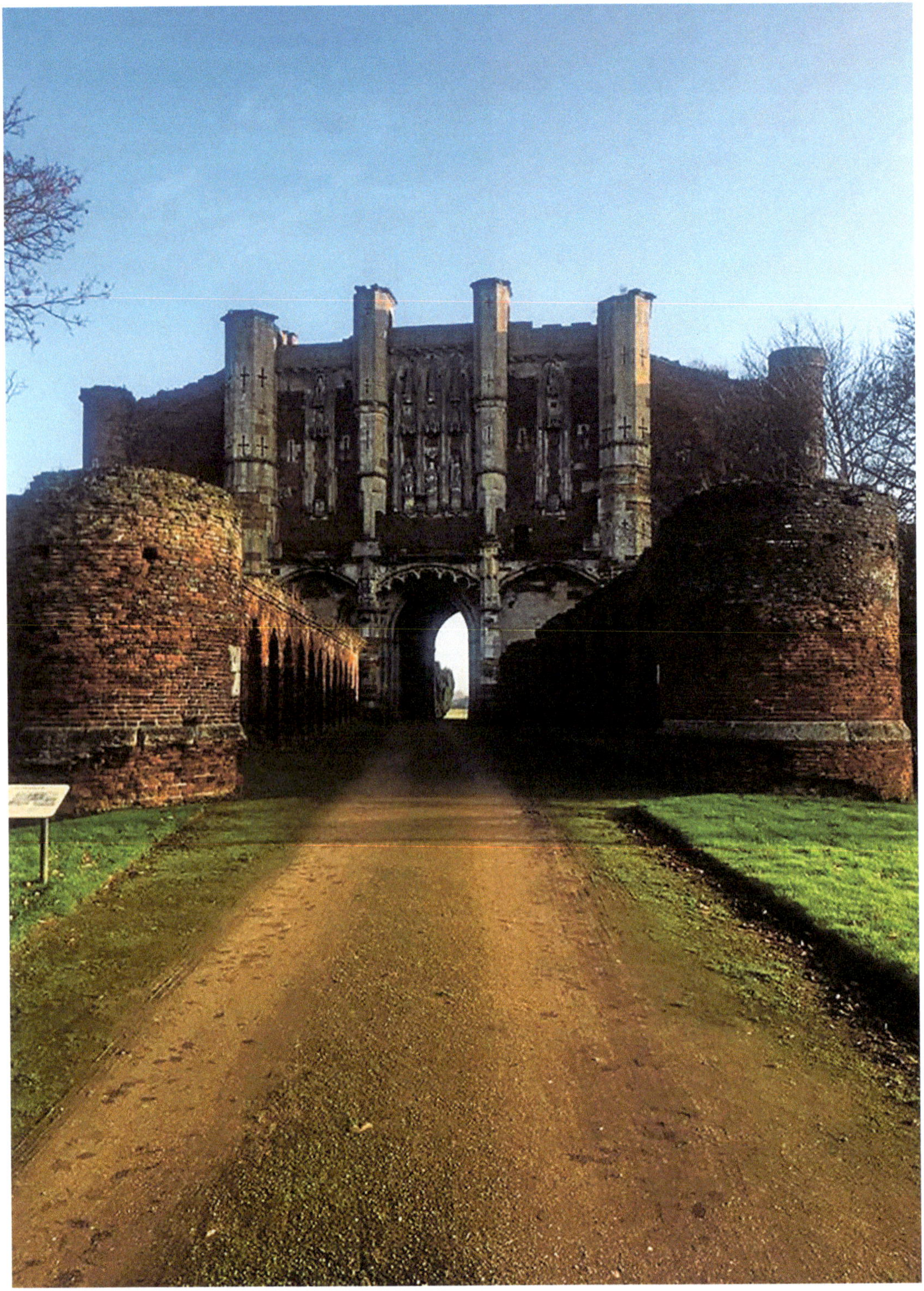

This fortress protects the outside of the abbey.

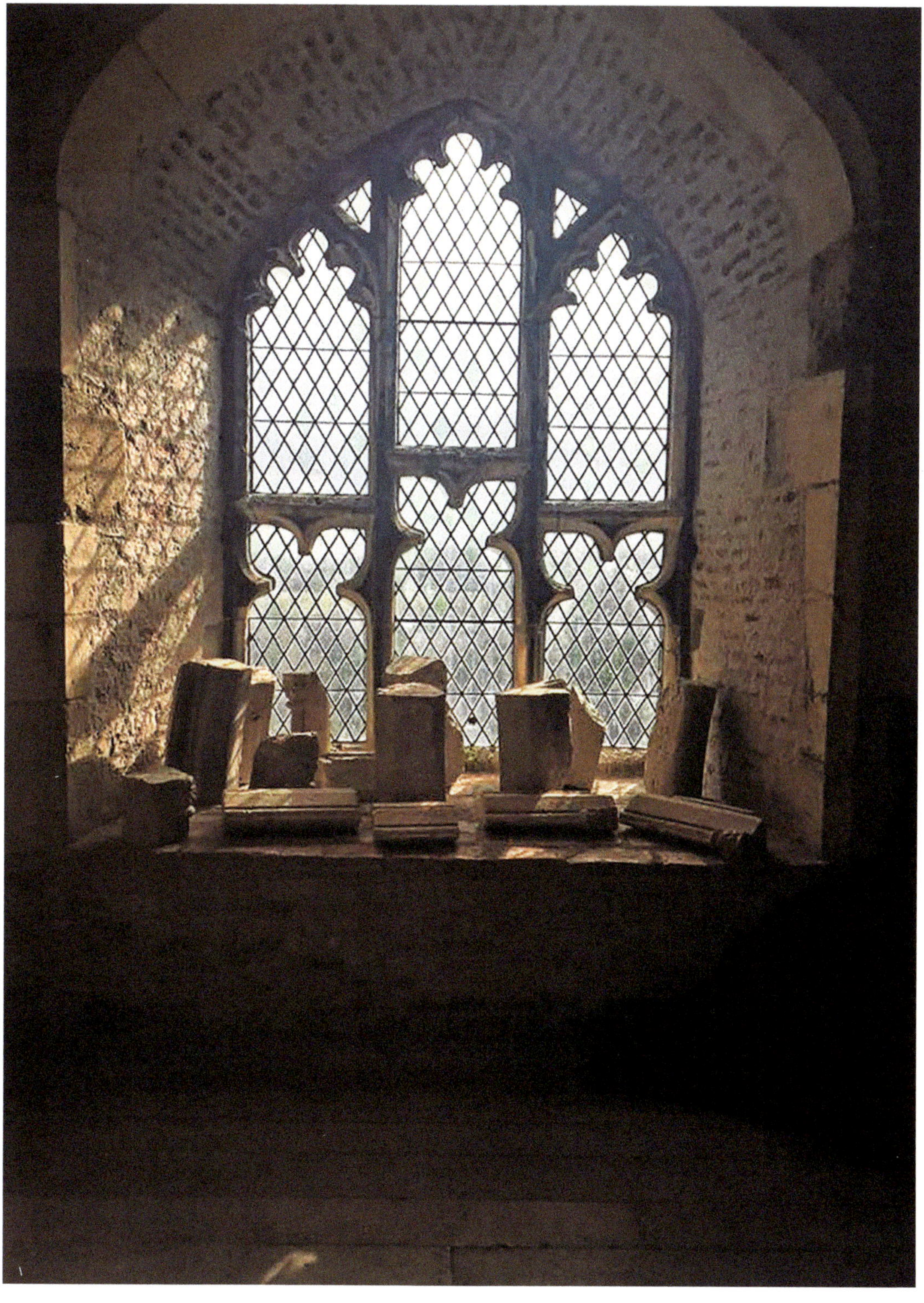

The abbey is open for all and maintained regularly.

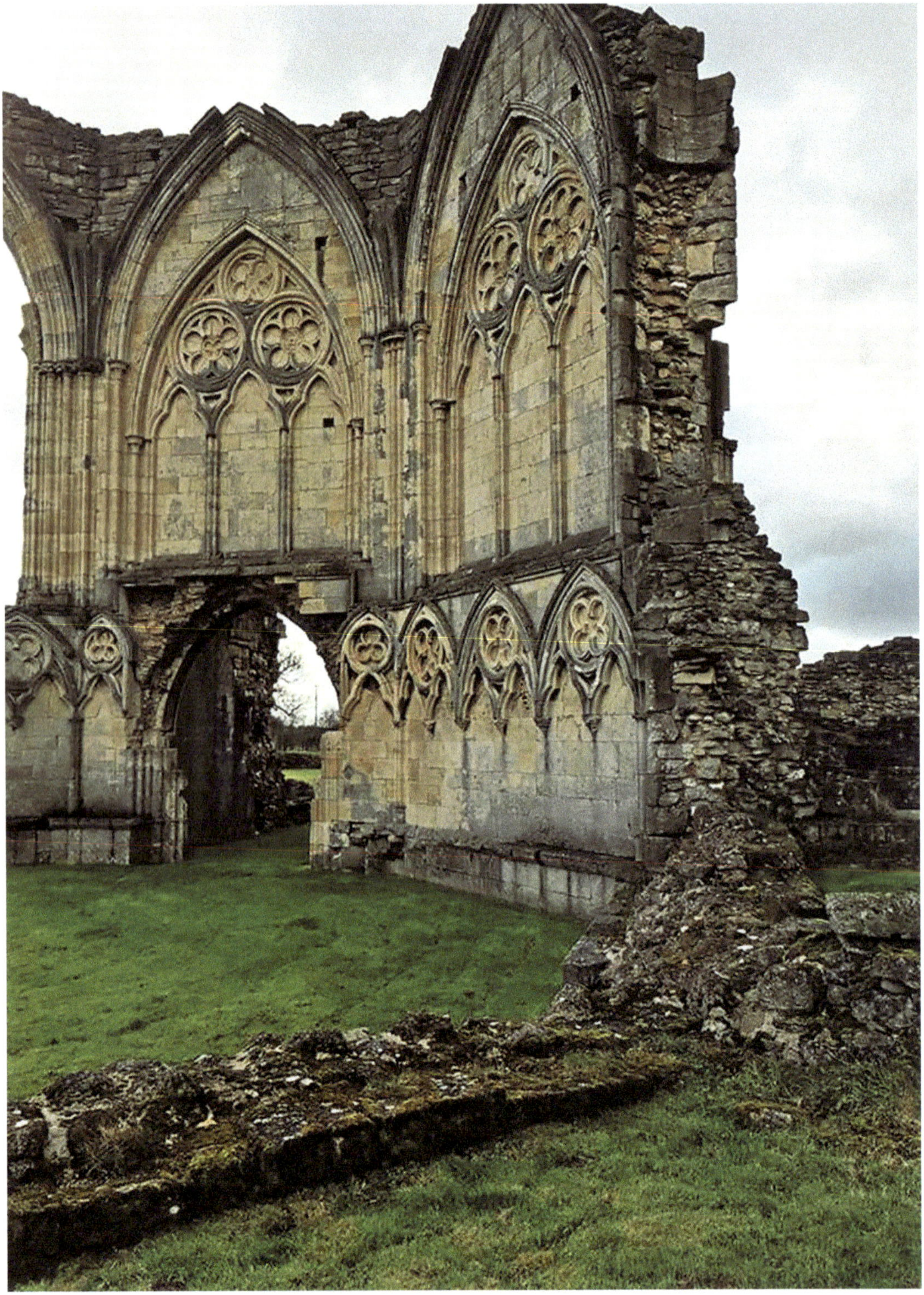

Ruins – perhaps one of the cloisters.

Behind the walls of the gatehouse lies a now destroyed octagonal chapter house. Though it is in ruins, the detail and basic structure is still intact for visitors to enjoy.

Much of the information on the abbey and its surroundings come from the Thornton Chronicle, which today is held in Oxford for safekeeping. The abbey was never completely demolished, though it was at severe risk when many monasteries were dissolved due to its revival. Henry VII also stayed on the grounds with Catherine Howard and was shortly after chosen as a place to train priests, a rather fortunate event despite its struggles.

While Scunthorpe features many Christian churches, making it very difficult choosing which to include within this book, it is important to not ignore places of worship that concern other religions. That being said, there are few religious places here compared with the number of Christian churches within the town, but the growth in the area's population has helped to encourage this range of diversity. Scunthorpe's central mosque is the largest and most popular in the area, and was established in 1981. The place of worship began simply as a housing property, but over time has expanded due to its growing influence in the area. Quite recently, the mosque held its annual Eid Mubarak festival, which was enjoyed by many in the Muslim community within Scunthorpe. The Islamic Centre is also a featured place of worship located on Parkinson Avenue, and an example of local Islamic influence as a number of venues have been set up in order to provide a location for convenient worship. Scunthorpe is also home to some Sikh temples, such as the International Sikh Complex, as well as many other smaller sets of religions that have a place to respect within the community.

It is perhaps only logical to begin to cover some famous localities of the Scunthorpe area by a link to the religious elements of the town. Scunthorpe is indeed home to some famous figures and individuals, who are frequently remembered today by dedication and some local knowledge.

John and the Wesley Family

John Wesley was the founder of Methodism, along with his brother Charles and their many sisters. The Wesleys' connection to the history of Scunthorpe is their origins in Epworth to the west of the town, just past the village of Belton facing in the direction of Doncaster. Epworth is historical in its nature and its population grew mostly during the mid- to late nineteenth century.

Methodism was a Protestant movement, concerning itself with a perfectionist branch that deals with the separation of man and church. The Salvationist movement is philosophical in its nature and considers what it means to refurbish individual's consciousness in order to serve a greater purpose.

The Wesleys were most known for their preaching, but in a rather unusual way. They partook preaching outside as to spread their word further and attract a wider audience to hear their speeches. While the idea of preaching outside may not seem unusual, it was the rallying of support and passionate force of it that attracted particular attention to the Wesley family.

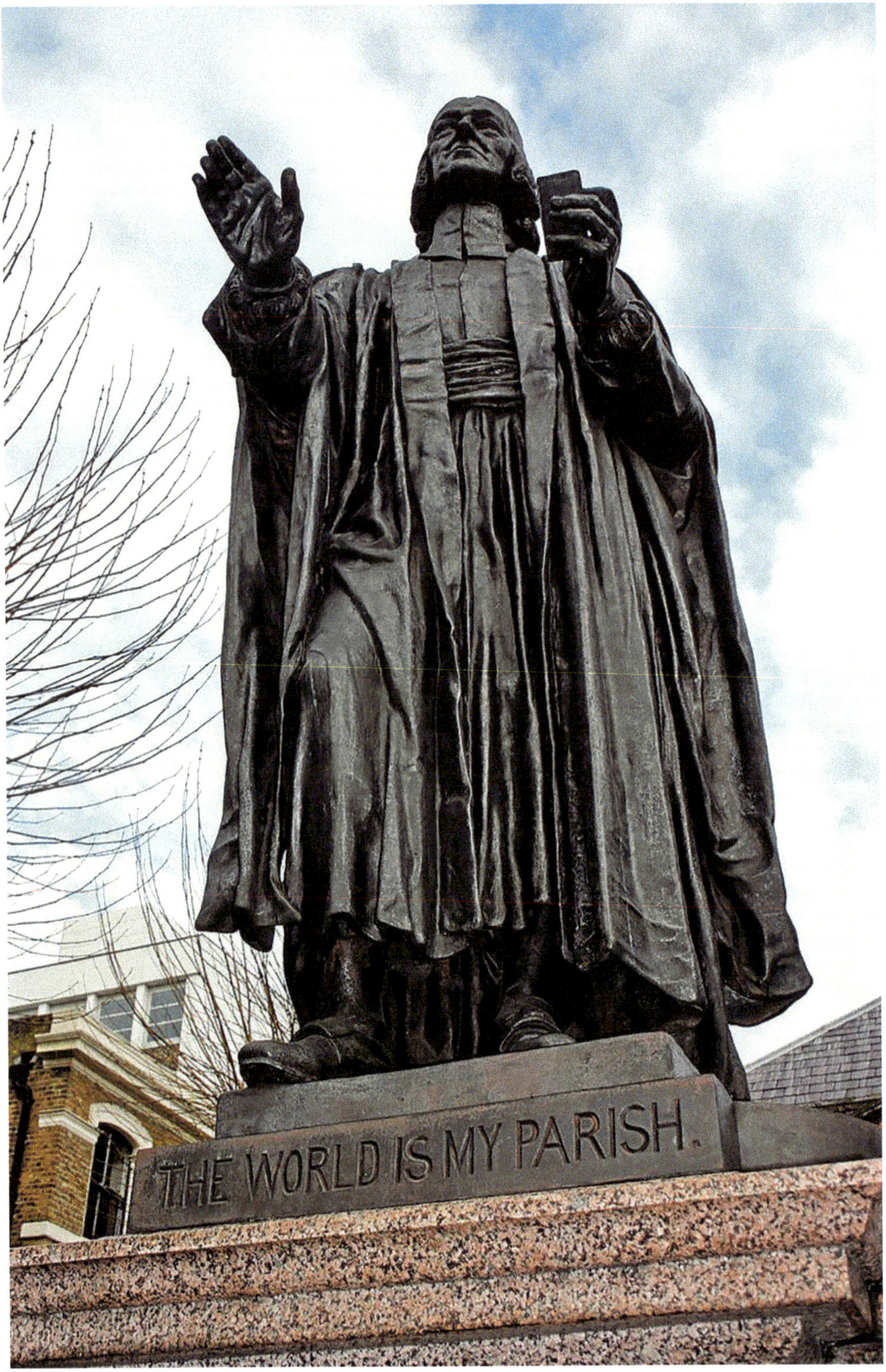

A statue of the most famous Wesley. (Courtesy of Mike Peel)

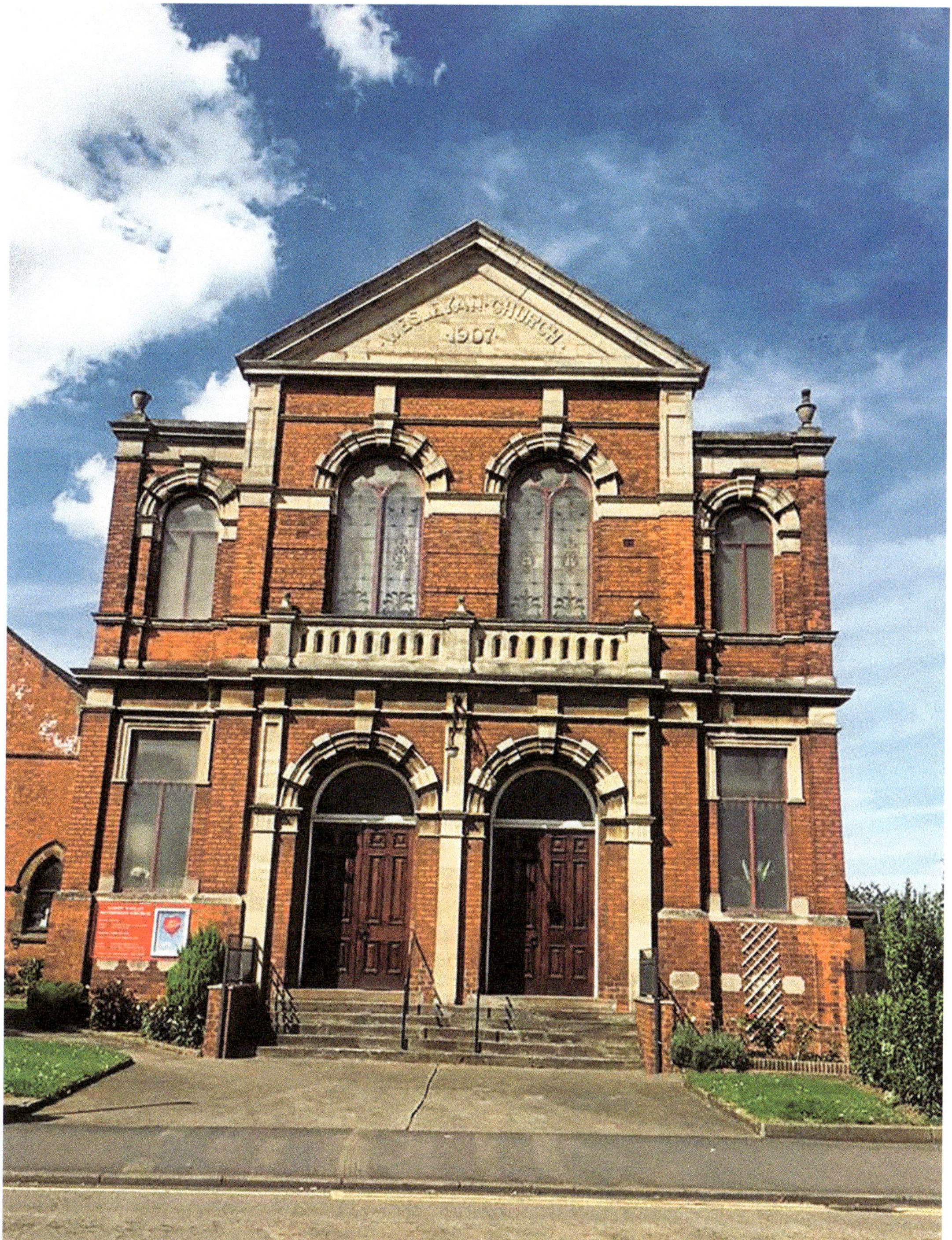

A church dedicated to the Wesley family and Methodism.

Rector Samuel Wesley of St Andrew's Church was the father of the Wesley family, and often partook in preaching within Epworth, but is widely known that this was not always met with joy. An alleged fire occurred at the Wesley household and, while the large family survived, it demonstrated that the word of his preaching would face potential opposition. Their former house was quickly rebuilt to become the grade one listed building today the Epworth Old Rectory, and is now open for people to visit.

DID YOU KNOW?

It has been reported that ghostly sightings are an occasional surprise at the Epworth Old Rectory. Some have allegedly seen one of the home's caretakers, while others have come into contact with some of the Wesley family members (though this should not put you off if you wish to visit the home).

The rectory was not only home to those who created and contributed towards the Methodist movement, but also to academic works that were circulated widely beyond Epworth. The death of Samuel was perhaps the birth of John Wesley's life of preaching; it is famously known that he preached on his father's grave shortly after his passing. His Oxford education served him well, like the rest of his family, travelling from place to place around England, Ireland, Scotland, and Wales to spread his gospel.

8. Scunthorpe Today: The Verge of its First Century

As we are soon approaching the town's first 100 since its initial formation, it is conceivably an opportunity to shine light upon the aspects of the area that are modern. The fact that the town will soon be a century old is not at all an exclusive reason to talk about the present events, but rather that we easily forget that those current happenings are history in the making. Though this chapter will not be what is considered a modern history update, it is instead a space to bring everything together, capturing some of those features that are almost passing through their phase to become 'history'. Not only this, but there are perhaps some topics within this section that tend to the town's uniqueness, while combining varied lesser-known aspects. This is not to suggest that other chapters have not had this same objective in mind, but this final chapter of Scunthorpe's history should, perhaps, reflect the pride that only a concluding section could achieve. The fondness of the town's markets, events and leisure industry deserve to be covered in a place that is dedicated to a concise encapsulation of Scunthorpe itself. From its slow start from the grounds of steel to the place an entire community lives today, Scunthorpe's pride is difficult to ignore.

Scunthorpe's Twin Towns

In most places, towns and cities are often twinned with other settlements in foreign countries but we give little thought to them. Scunthorpe is twinned with the towns

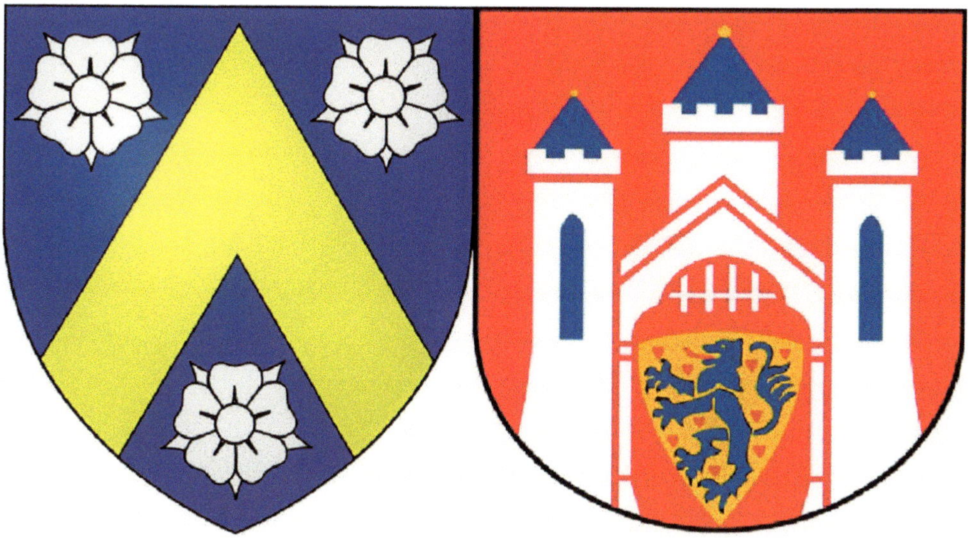

The two shields of Scunthorpe's twin towns.

of Luneburg (located in Germany, near to Hamburg) and Clamart (on the outskirts of Paris).

There are many reasons for towns to be twinned together, though it is mainly thought to encourage economic and social integration between foreign countries.

The Lincolnshire Flag

For quite some time, I would travel from village to village around Scunthorpe and see that many people had a colourful flag flying from flagpoles or simply a shed roof. This flag turned out to actually be the flag of Lincolnshire and has been in use since 2005 when Michelle Andrews designed and won part of a competition to create a new flag for the county. Though the competition was won by a voting system, the reason for the development of a new flag was a mechanism designed to increase tourism and visitors into the Lincolnshire area. Though many people associate the county simply with the local capital of Lincoln, its actual size is large and boarders a number of other established counties such as Yorkshire and Nottinghamshire. What stands out the most about the flag is the representation of the county, and is arguably the reason why the flag was chosen to represent the pride of Lincolnshire. The colours depict the labouring nature

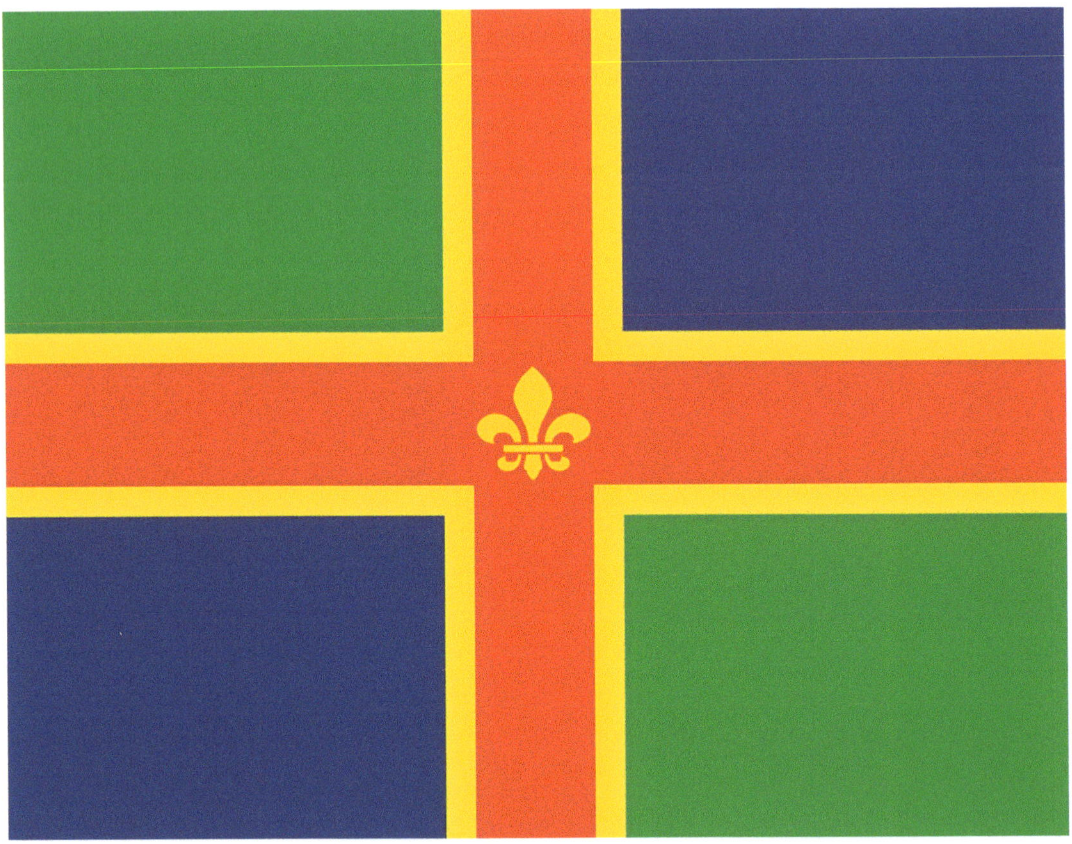

The winning flag, representing the colours of the county.

and opportunities of the land; for example, the yellow and green represent the fertility of the green landscape to crow plentiful crops. The blue is quite obviously set to show the influence of the sea, as a result of bordering the end of the land, the seaside towns of Skegness and Mablethorpe are another unique feature of the Lincolnshire county.

DID YOU KNOW?
Scunthorpe's official coat of arms features a typical green shield and knight's helmet. But what people often don't notice is the blast furnace at the top, representing the importance of the steel industry within the town.

The Royal Visit to Scunthorpe

As part of a national visit to the counties of England by the royal family, the Queen and Prince Philip travelled to a few of Lincolnshire towns, including Lincoln itself, Grimsby, and Scunthorpe. The royals visited Lincoln Cathedral and Grimsby Docks before they travelled to Scunthorpe and watched the Frodingham ironworks operate and create its renowned industrial output. The event was so significant in the town that crowds lined up at the barriers to watch the Queen's car drive through the town. The annual gala produced a special mug for the occasion that same year.

Scunthorpe's Gala

The presence of the annual gala may still linger in the memories for those who have lived in Scunthorpe for even a short amount of time. The event was set up after the First World War and dedicated to all of the children in the town, not just those who had parents working within the steel industry. Perhaps the existence was partly to compensate for the long working hours at the steelworks and therefore provided a place for enjoyment for all families. The gala traditionally took place at Normanby. Though it does not unfortunately run anymore, similar events have taken place near to Central Park as part of an effort to reinstate it.

DID YOU KNOW?
The annual gala would gift those that attended an identical mug that would change year on year. Many have kept these, and recent attempts of galas similar to the traditional one have stuck by this tradition. There were even special ones for royal weddings and anniversaries!

The Markets

As discussed previously in this book, it was perhaps the case that the town centre had not always been originally planned to exist where it is today. In a similar notion, the markets of the town – one at the town centre and one at Ashby – may bear witness to this concept of bustling areas and a struggle to determine where to create business for all. The markets

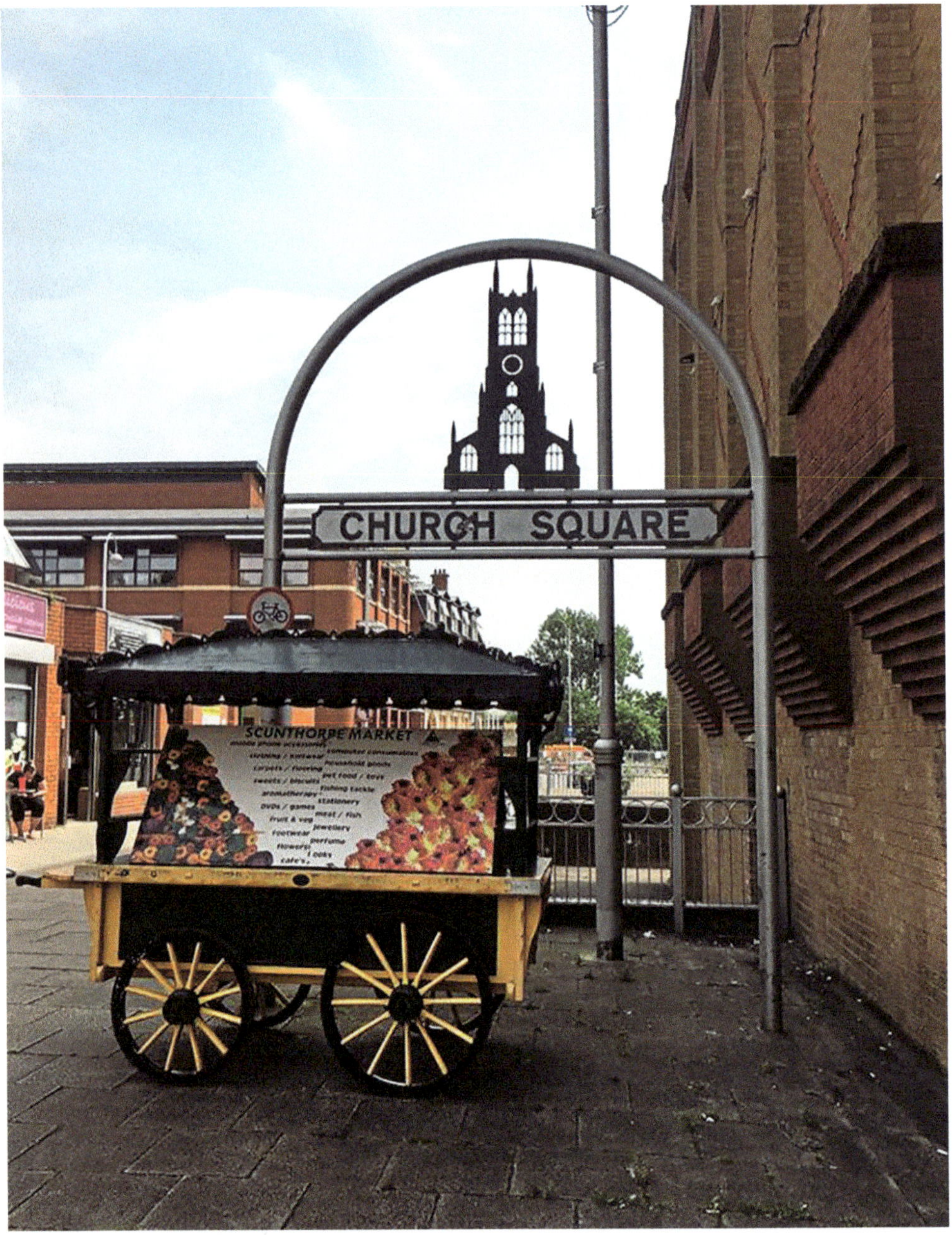

The town's Square is home to the Saturday market.

of Scunthorpe are historic in their nature and were designed to cater to the demands of the villages. Ashby tends to both Bottesford's and Yaddlethorpe's needs as well as its own, while the market based in the town centre supplies goods for those across Brumby and Crosby.

Ashby market was remodelled in 1970 to make it easier for consumers to shop at their own leisure. The market based at the town centre, often known as simply 'Scunthorpe Market', is a place many remember having rides outside for children to play on.

The Majestic Cinema

The classic cinema was formerly known as one of the town's treasures, and even today the old pictures of the venue attract many enthusiasts. Located on the corner of Oswald Road and Mary Street, it was in a prime spot to attract visitors and excited customers waiting to watch its latest film release. Though the cinema certainly was one of Scunthorpe's highlights the eighty years it was functioning, it went through a whirlwind of ownerships as a way to produce better business results and a greater average revenue. Unfortunately, the cinema was demolished in 2007; the land is now left available, though little construction has since taken place.

Brigg's Annual Fair

On 5 August each year, for over 100 years, Brigg fair has been running to revive the classical sense of its animal trading and exchange of produce in the old market town.

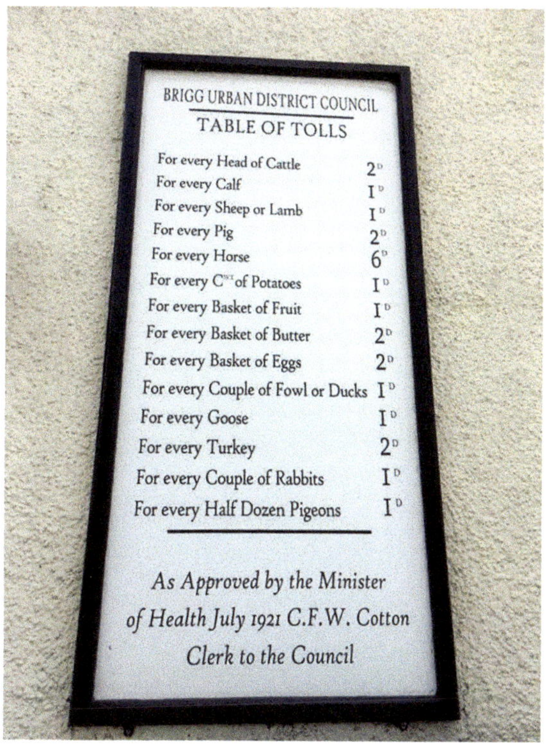

The units have remained unchanged since the fair began.

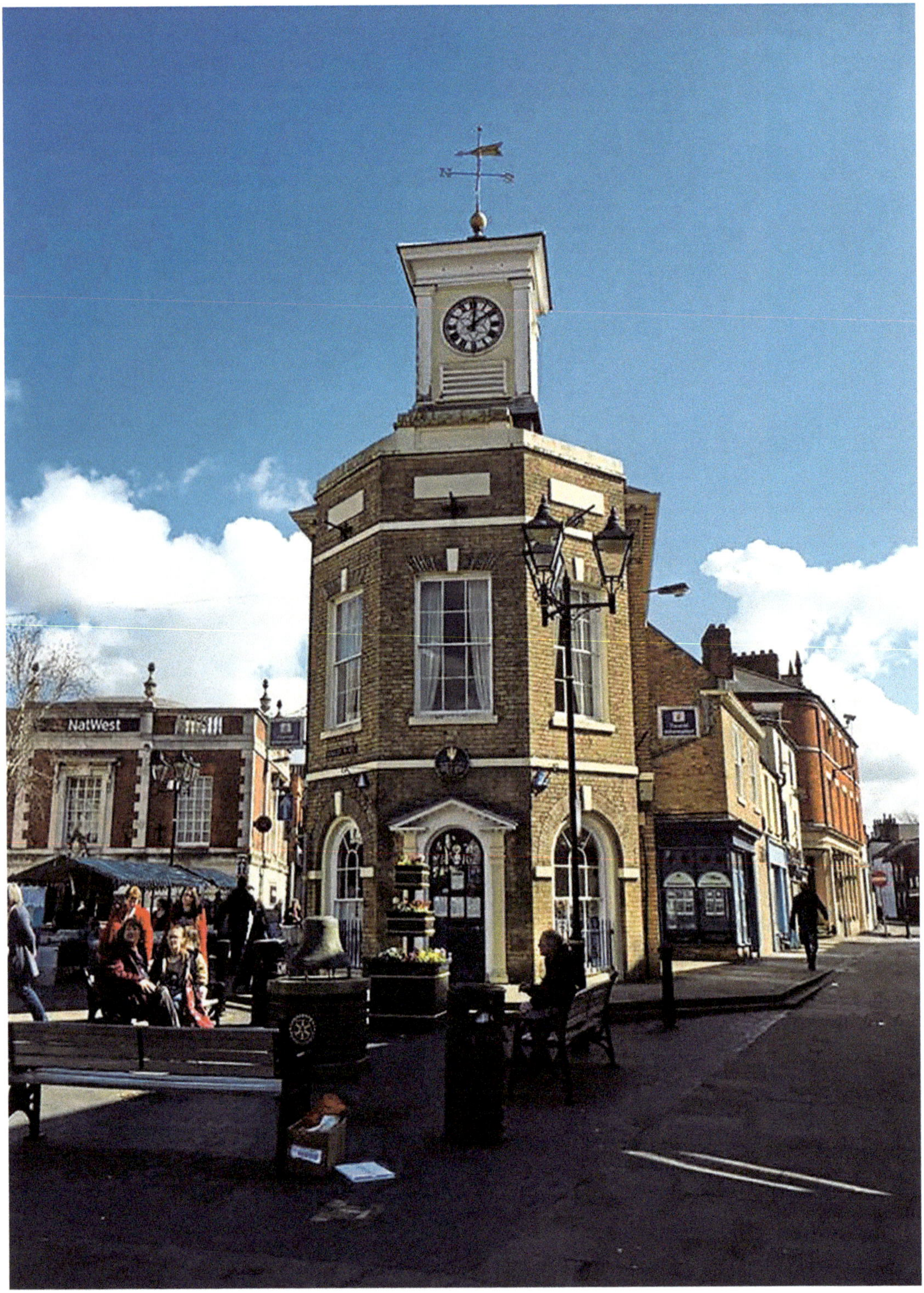

Brigg today.

Even though the fair runs only for one day, the toll boards that can be found at opposite ends of the small town centre and have been restored with the original currency prices of livestock. What perhaps makes the fair more unique is the song 'Brigg Fair' that was written as a dedication to the market. Though this is not at all unheard of (for example, 'Scarborough Fair') the small size of the market town makes the whole idea much more original, as well as being the theme at the market every year.

The Skyscraper Scene

If you are travelling into the town from the west entrance of the motorway, the first 'skyscraper' of Scunthorpe is always visible on the horizon. More commonly known as Westcliff flats, Trent View House was constructed in 1963 in attempt to create a vision of a modernistic urban town while providing a suitable place for residents to live with a view. The view from the flats stretch over to the villages of Burringham and Keadby, as well as the motorway leading to the town.

A second block of flats were built in the town centre, though unfortunately the countryside view could not be equally achieved from every location in Scunthorpe.

Party in the Pines: Its Last Festival

The small festival is a familiar social event for many who do not even attend the camping event in summer. Often based during late summer, the event includes music and camping in the preserved woodland area next to the Forest Pines Resort near the village of Broughton. The festival has been running for a number of years and has attracted much attention since its start; its focus is particularly based on small local bands and artists. Due to the environmental side, this year was its last year running as Party in the Pines.

The Tour of Britain Passed Through North Lincolnshire

The bike tour that took place in early September 2017 passed though the surrounding village of Scunthorpe as part of one of its stages in order to access the North of England. The tour is a staged race that takes place over a number of consecutive days, though it is particularly exciting for local residents that the tour involves the area. In celebration of this, some of the villages have participated in an activity whereby bikes have been painted bright colours and stationed around the central points in the community. Some of these can be seen at Messingham, but also in the small villages surrounding Brigg.

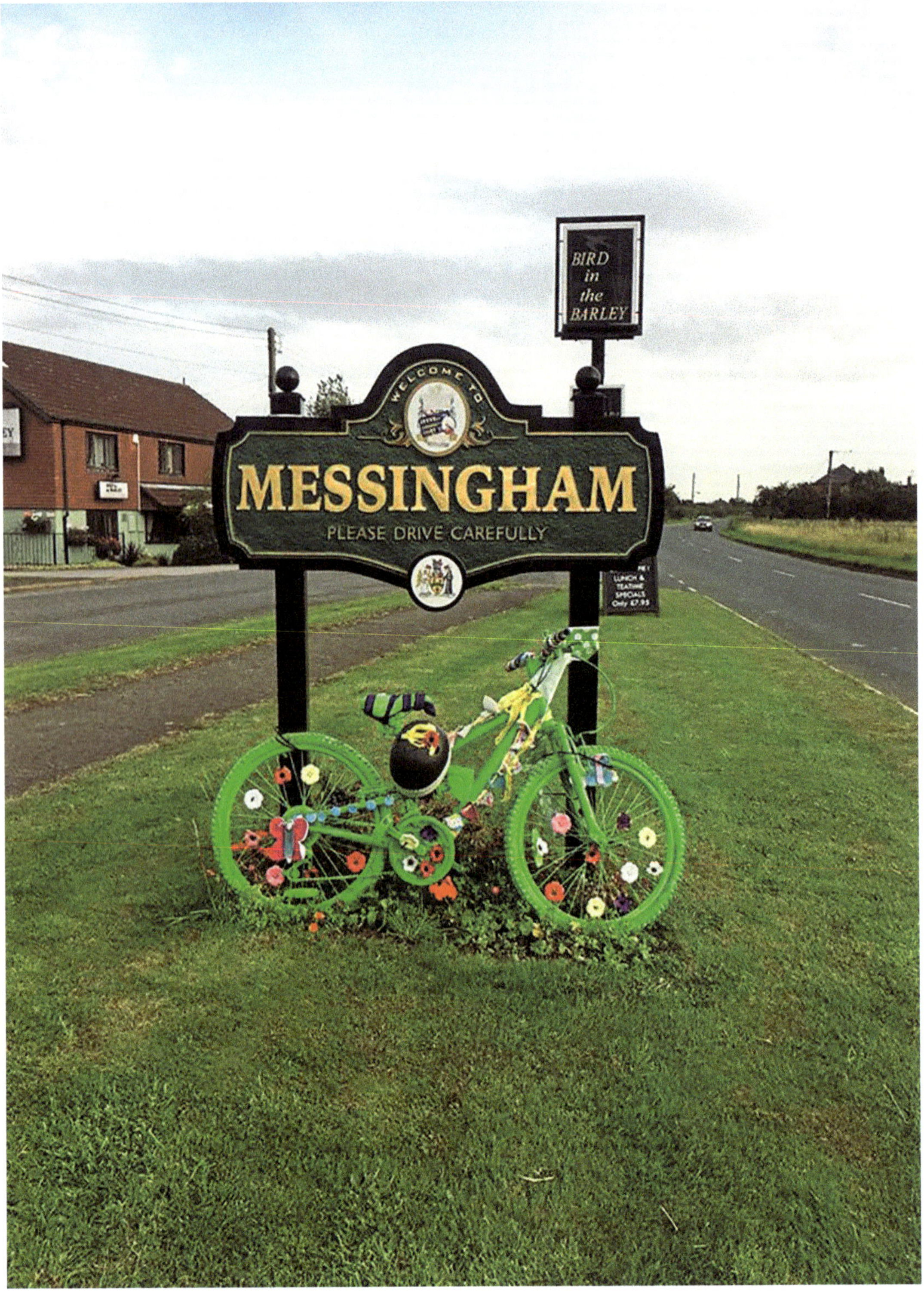

Colourful bikes were stationed all over the town for the Tour of Britain in 2017.

A Final Word

To most, Scunthorpe is simply a small town 'up North'. But to me and many other people it will always be home. While writing this, I struggled not only to apprehend how long the settlement of modern Scunthorpe has been in existance, but the depth to which the history lies. I believe that the hours spent writing, researching and engaging with the setting of Scunthorpe has made me prouder and closer with the town. It is perhaps a duty to all of us to challenge anyone that tells us where we come from is not significant.

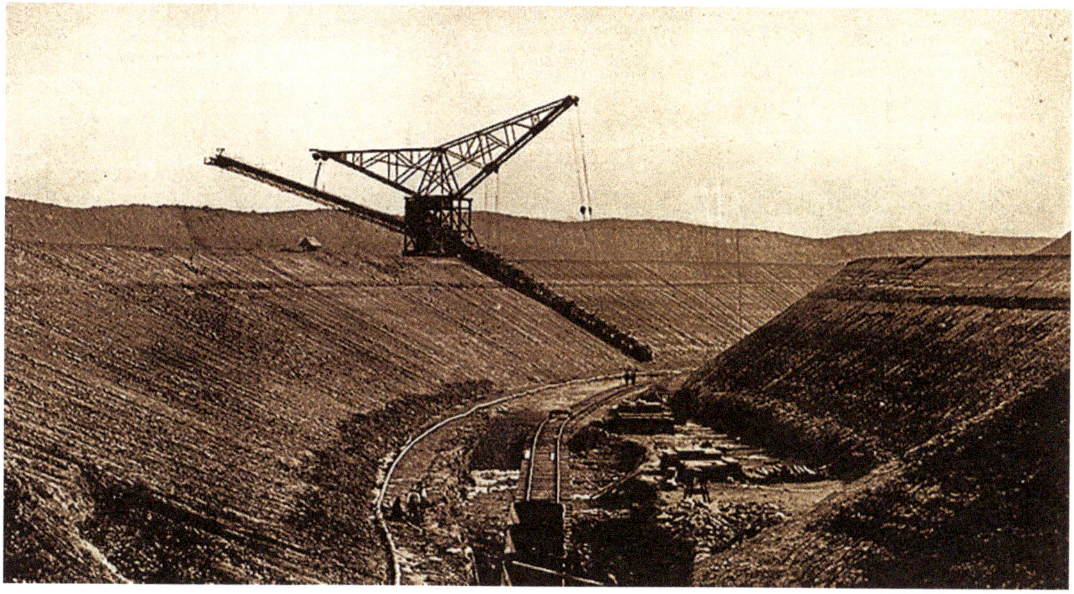

The making of steel, Scunthorpe's purpose.

Notes

1. The Winterton Lady can be found in the North Lincolnshire Museum, Scunthorpe, along with many artefacts found from excavations on nearly all of these historical periods.
2. A quote from one of the workers in the book *Steeltown*.
3. Yaddlethorpe is a small village or district joined to Bottesford and Scunthorpe.
4. From the 'History of the Church' section supplied on the website for the visual arts centre.

Bibliography

Creed, R. and Coult, A., *Steeltown: The Real Life Drama of the Men and Women Who Built an Industry* (The Hutton Press Ltd: Beverley, 1990).

Hatch, F. H., *The Iron and Steel Industry of the United Kingdom under War Conditions* (1919).

Leadby, Kevin and Couts, Catherine M., *The Lost Kingdom: The Search for Anglo-Saxon Lindsey* (Scunthorpe Borough Museums & Art Gallery, 1987).

Leahy, Kevin, *The Anglo-Saxon Kingdom of Lindsey* (Tempus Publishing: Chalford, 2007).

Longbone, Bryan, *Steam and Steel: An Illustrated History of Scunthorpe's Railways* (Irwell Press: Gwynedd, 1996).

May, Jeffrey, *Prehistoric Lincolnshire: History of Lincolnshire Volume I* (The History of Lincolnshire Committee: Lincoln, 1976).

Owen, Dorothy M., *Church and Society in Medieval Lincolnshire: History of Lincolnshire Volume V* (The History of Lincolnshire Committee: Lincoln, 1981).

Peach, Howard, *The Curiosities of England: Lincolnshire Curiosities* (Dovecote Press Ltd: Dorset, 1994).

Staff, John, *From Nuts to Iron: The Official History of Scunthorpe United 1899–2012* (4 edge Limited).

Taylor, David J., 'I Remember Normanby…', in *Life on a Lincolnshire Estate Between the Wars* (Scunthorpe Museums and the Hutton Press Ltd: Beverly, 1994).

Wright, Neil R., *Lincolnshire Towns and Industry 1700–1914: History of Lincolnshire Volume XI* (History of Lincolnshire Committee: Lincoln, 1982).

Acknowledgements

Thank you to Scunthorpe Library, Brigg Heritage Centre and the North Lincolnshire Museum for supplying amazing resources that have helped form the basis for this book. Thank you also to my parents and close friends for their invaluable support. Thanks also go to: Alkborough Maze Committee; Andrew Brown for talking with me about Appleby and the railways, who is part of the WEA group in Scunthorpe; Appleby Frodingham Railway Preservation Society; British Steel PLC; English Heritage; Kay for chatting with me on the history of Brigg at the Heritage Centre; Members of Scunthorpe Memories Group; Nazsidhu from Rowland Road Convenience for your information on the local area; North Lincolnshire Council; staff of St Lawrence Church; staff of St Hugh's Church; those customers and staff at The Berkeley, High Field House and the Malt Shovel who were happy to take the time to share your knowledge and stories about the pubs; and Nos 20–21 Visual Arts Centre.